SWA

Secrets of

AGA PUDDINGS

LUCY YOUNG

Secrets of
AGA PUDDINGS
LUCY YOUNG

EBURY
PRESS

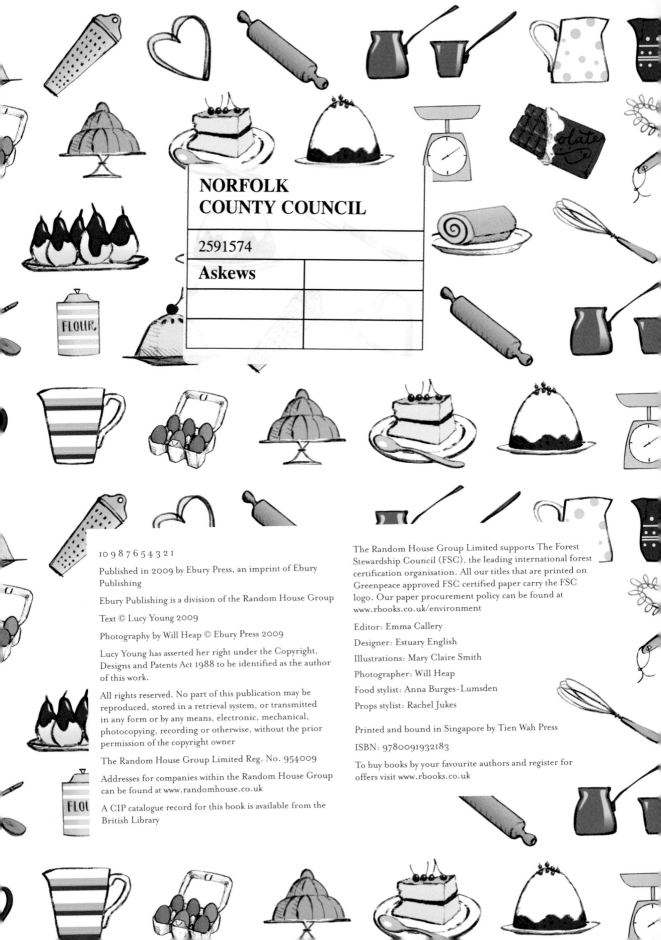

**NORFOLK
COUNTY COUNCIL**

2591574

Askews

10 9 8 7 6 5 4 3 2 1

Published in 2009 by Ebury Press, an imprint of Ebury Publishing

Ebury Publishing is a division of the Random House Group

The Random House Group Limited Reg. No. 954009

Addresses for companies within the Random House Group can be found at www.randomhouse.co.uk

A CIP catalogue record for this book is available from the British Library

The Random House Group Limited supports The Forest Stewardship Council (FSC), the leading international forest certification organisation. All our titles that are printed on Greenpeace approved FSC certified paper carry the FSC logo. Our paper procurement policy can be found at www.rbooks.co.uk/environment

Editor: Emma Callery
Designer: Estuary English
Illustrations: Mary Claire Smith
Photographer: Will Heap
Food stylist: Anna Burges-Lumsden
Props stylist: Rachel Jukes

Printed and bound in Singapore by Tien Wah Press

ISBN: 9780091932183

To buy books by your favourite authors and register for offers visit www.rbooks.co.uk

Contents

Mary Berry

This is the first and only illustrated book dedicated to making puddings in the Aga. Lucy has meticulously tested each and every recipe, giving instructions for 2, 3 and 4 oven Agas. I have been lucky enough to share many of these wonderful creations as Lucy brings them in to me when we work together — those days are special even after 20 years of working together.

Lucy know all the tricks of the trade relating to cooking with an Aga. From her years of giving Aga demonstrations she is an expert at giving clear advice, with foolproof recipes, and each recipe has a 'secret' — a coveted tip, giving you the perfect results. She uses the Aga to its full advantage, from the simplest Fresh Strawberry Soufflé and decadent Mocha Mousse Cake to the stunning Lemon Shortbread with Lemon Curd and Summer Fruits, just to mention a few. There is no pudding you cannot make in the Aga, and the wonderful variety of recipes gives something for every occasion.

Everyone who owns an Aga should make a place for this modern, classic book in their kitchen.

Introduction

This is the first Aga book dedicated to puddings and desserts. It is packed full of new, modern recipes, and includes some of your favourites too. Puddings and baking are well and truly back in fashion, more people are cooking at home and when asking people about their favourite puddings, the old classics always come top of the list. Try Luxury Lemon Bread and Butter Pudding (see page 24), Divine Chocolate and Peppermint Mousse (see page 126) or even Double Apple Galette (see page 44) for some new ideas.

Whatever the occasion, I am sure that you will find a suitable recipe within these pages. Furthermore, this book shows you that puddings can be a triumph when cooked in the Aga and need not be complicated or stressful. As with my *Secrets of Aga Cakes* book, I have kept the process as simple as possible to make the recipes foolproof, with additional Secrets to guide you through the recipe and give you tips on technique.

This book was a pleasure to write; not great for my waistline, but my friends and family enjoyed their share and there is no better way to put a smile on someone's face than to give them a delicious pudding! When I am cooking for friends I usually give the option of a naughty pudding and fresh fruit, so in this book there is a selection of both. All recipes have conventional instructions too, so *Secrets of Aga Puddings* is perfect as a gift for a non-Aga friend too.

I am sure you will enjoy the recipes I've created for you among these pages and remember that a small slice of something delicious is better than a large slice of something low fat and tasteless!

Lucy Young

AGA COOKING TIPS

Below are general Aga tips so if you are new to using the Aga, this helps with the Aga know-how. To get the perfect results, always cook in the right sized tin and correct oven position.

THE AGA

- Boiling plate is the left top plate.
- Simmering plate is the right top plate.
- Two-oven Aga: the top oven is the roasting oven and the bottom oven is the simmering oven.
- Three-oven Aga: the top oven is the roasting oven, bottom right is the simmering oven and bottom left is the baking oven.
- Four-oven Aga: the top right is the roasting oven, top left is the simmering oven, bottom right is the baking oven and bottom left is the warming oven.
- The grid shelf is the ridged shelf that comes with the Aga and stays in the oven.
- The cold sheet is the sheet that comes free with your Aga, a flat metal sheet the size of the ovens. This stays out of the Aga so it is always cold and is used to blank off the heat from the top of the oven to prevent the recipe from burning.

GENERAL TIPS

- Remember that all Agas are different, so timings may vary slightly.
- Write in the book any changes to the timings, so you know for next time.
- Re-conditioned Agas have cooler simmering ovens.
- Weigh accurately and follow the recipe exactly for perfect results.
- Weigh in either imperial or metric measures, do not mix the two.

- Cook in the correct position stated in the recipe.
- When a 'runner' is mentioned in a recipe, e.g. 'slide on to the second set of runners', they are counted from the top.

EQUIPMENT

All the cooking equipment used in this book is standard equipment that most of you will have at home. I have also used Aga equipment, which you get free with your Aga or is available in Aga shops. I try not to use specialised equipment – I am a home cook, not a chef! It is important to use the right sized tin or dish as otherwise the cooking time may be affected. Remember when mixing or whisking that the larger the bowl and whisk, the easier it is to mix.

INGREDIENTS

All the ingredients in this book can be easily bought from your local supermarket. If I cannot buy it easily, I will not put it in a book – no special delivery ordering, just ingredients that are easy to buy and accessible to all. Buy the very best ingredients that you can afford, buy fruit in season and buy British where possible to support our local farmers.

- All eggs are large unless stated otherwise. Try to use free-range, if possible and bear in mind that eggs only need to be at room temperature when being used for whisking. It is fine to use eggs from the fridge for everything else.
- All fruit are medium sized and ripe, unless stated otherwise.
- I use Bournville chocolate for all my recipes (except truffles) as I find it foolproof to melt and less sugar is added.

Rainy day puddings

These are timeless and traditional desserts – exactly the kind of warming treat that your mother and grandmother used to make. The perfect pick me up they are the ultimate comfort food to indulge in on a rainy day.

HALF-TIME RUM AND CHERRY DESSERTS

Lovely Lucinda, who helps me test recipes and give demonstrations, gave me the idea for this recipe as she ate something similar at half-time while watching her football team at their stadium. She wanted me to name the recipe after her team but I can't bring myself to do it as they are the London rivals of my Man U, favourites! Not suitable for freezing.

- Serves 6

1 x 435 g can black pitted cherries in fruit juice	110 g (4 oz) self-raising flour
	1/2 tsp baking powder
6 heaped tsp cherry jam	For the rum syrup
2 eggs	75 g (3 oz) caster sugar
110 g (4 oz) butter, softened	2 tbsp dark rum
110 g (4 oz) caster sugar	

You will need six size 1 (150 ml/¼ pint) ramekins, greased.

Drain the cherries, reserving the fruit juice and divide the cherries equally between the bases of the ramekins. Spoon one heaped teaspoon of cherry jam on top of the cherries in each of the ramekins.

Measure the eggs, butter, sugar, self-raising flour and baking powder into a mixing bowl and beat with a wooden spoon or hand-held electric mixer, until smooth. Divide the sponge between the ramekins and level the tops. Sit the ramekins on a baking sheet.

TWO-OVEN AGA Slide on to the grid shelf on the floor of the roasting oven with the cold sheet on the second set of runners. Cook for 25–30 minutes, until golden and risen.

THREE- AND FOUR-OVEN AGA Slide on to the grid shelf on the floor of the baking oven. Cook for 30 minutes, until golden and risen. If it starts getting too brown, slide the cold sheet on to the second set of runners.

CONVENTIONAL OVEN Bake in a preheated oven (180°C/160°C Fan/Gas 4) for 30 minutes, until golden and risen.

Meanwhile, make the syrup. Measure the reserved fruit juice into a saucepan with the sugar and gently dissolve the sugar on the simmering plate (or hob), stirring. Boil on the boiling plate (or turn up the heat on the hob) for 4–5 minutes, until it is syrupy and measures about 75 ml (3 fl oz). Add the rum to the pan.

Leave the sponges to cool for about 5 minutes, loosen with a palette knife around the edges and turn out on to plates or a serving dish. Pour the hot syrup over the puddings and serve immediately.

Secret

- The sponge is very sweet and sticky due to the syrup, but with the cherries and rum is similar to rum baba.

STEAMED SYRUP PUDDING

This is a classic recipe, perfect for a rainy day Sunday lunch. Not suitable for freezing.

- Serves 6

> 8 tbsp golden syrup
> 2 tbsp lemon juice
> 175 g (6 oz) butter, softened
> 175 g (6 oz) caster sugar
> 3 eggs
> 175 g (6 oz) self-raising flour
> Finely grated zest of 1 lemon
> 3 tbsp milk

You will need a 1 litre (1¾ lb) pudding basin, greased.

For the topping, mix together the syrup and lemon juice and pour into the base of the pudding basin.

Measure the remaining ingredients into a mixing bowl and whisk with a hand-held electric mixer, until combined. Pour the pudding mixture into the basin. Then put a lid on the basin or cut a piece of foil to fit (see secret).

Sit the basin in a deep saucepan with a tight fitting lid. Pour boiling water into the pan so it comes three-quarters of the way up the side of the basin. Cover the saucepan with a lid.

TWO-, THREE- AND FOUR-OVEN AGA Bring to the boil on the boiling plate and continue to boil on the simmering plate for about 5 minutes. Transfer to the simmering oven for 1½–2 hours, until the sponge is firm and cooked.

CONVENTIONAL OVEN Bring to the boil on the hob and boil for about 5 minutes. Lower the heat and simmer for about 2 hours, until firm and cooked – top up the water if necessary.

Carefully remove the lid or foil, turn upside down on top of a plate and serve warm with cream or custard.

Secret

- You can now buy plastic basins with lids, which are perfect for this recipe. But if you only have an earthenware basin, make a foil lid. Cut a circle about 5 cm (2 in) bigger than the basin, make a pleat in the top and grease the underside with butter. Sit it on top of the basin and seal the edges tightly around the rim so no steam escapes.

MAGIC LEMON SPONGE PUDDING

This is a classic recipe where the cooked lemon sponge has a thin layer of lemon sauce at the bottom of the dish – I have added a modern twist of lemon curd. Not suitable for freezing.

- Serves 6

> 110 g (4 oz) butter, softened
> 110 g (4 oz) caster sugar
> 4 eggs, separated
> 50 g (2 oz) plain flour
> 2 tbsp good quality lemon curd (or see Luxury Lemon Curd on page 153)
> Finely grated zest and juice of 2 lemons
> 300 ml (½ pint) milk

You will need a 1.5 litre (2½ pint) wide based shallow ovenproof dish, greased.

Measure the butter and sugar into a bowl and whisk with a hand-held electric mixer, until light and fluffy. Add the egg yolks, flour, lemon curd, lemon zest and juice and whisk again, slowly adding the milk while continuously whisking (it may look a little curdled, but don't worry).

Whisk the egg whites in another bowl until stiff and cloud-like. Mix one tablespoon of egg whites into the lemon mixture and then fold in the remaining egg whites, keeping the mixture light and fluffy. Spoon into the prepared dish.

TWO-OVEN AGA Slide on to the grid shelf on the floor of the roasting oven with the cold sheet on the second set of runners. Bake for 30 minutes, until well risen, lightly golden and firm to the touch in the centre.

THREE- AND FOUR-OVEN AGA Slide on to the grid shelf on the floor of the baking oven. Bake for 35–40 minutes, until well risen, lightly golden and firm to the touch in the centre.

CONVENTIONAL OVEN Bake in a preheated oven (190°C/170°C Fan/Gas 5) for about 40 minutes, until well risen, lightly golden and firm to the touch in the centre.

Serve at once with cream.

Secrets

- Use a wide open-topped ovenproof dish rather than a deep one so you get a lot of lovely golden topping.

- The sponge is quite soufflé-like with the addition of the egg whites, so be sure to fold them in carefully so no air is knocked out as otherwise the pudding will be dense and heavy.

STICKY TOFFEE PUDDING

This wonderful pudding has to be one of the all-time favourites. I make mine as a traybake, so the cooking time is slightly shorter than most, which is more suitable for the Aga. Cut it into squares and pour over the sauce – it looks so scrummy. Freezes well without the sauce.

- Serves 8–10. For the sponge

  75 g (3 oz) butter, softened
  175 g (6 oz) light soft brown sugar
  2 tsp bicarbonate of soda
  I tsp ground ginger
  225 g (8 oz) self-raising flour
  2 eggs
  2 tbsp treacle
  250 ml (8 fl oz) milk

- For the toffee sauce

  225 g (8 oz) soft light brown sugar
  110 g (4 oz) butter
  300 ml (½ pint) double cream

You will need a small Aga roasting tin or traybake tin measuring 30 x 23 cm (12 x 9 in). Cut a rectangle of non-stick baking parchment just larger than the base and sides of the tin and cut each corner with scissors to the depth of the tin. Grease the tin with butter and then line with the baking parchment, pushing it neatly into the corners to fit.

Measure all the sponge ingredients in a bowl and whisk with a hand-held electric mixer, until smooth. Spoon into the lined roasting tin.

TWO-OVEN AGA Slide on to the grid shelf on the floor of the roasting oven with the cold sheet on the second set of runners. Bake for about 25 minutes, until firm on top and shrinking around the edges.

THREE- AND FOUR-OVEN AGA Slide on to the grid shelf on the floor of the baking oven. Bake for about 30 minutes, until firm on top and shrinking around the edges. If it starts to become too dark, slide the cold sheet on to the second set of runners.

CONVENTIONAL OVEN Bake in a preheated oven (180°C/160°C Fan/Gas 4) for 30–35 minutes, until firm on top and shrinking around the edges. If it starts to become too dark, cover with foil.

For the sauce, measure all the ingredients into a pan and heat on the simmering plate (or hob), stirring until smooth. Then let it boil for a couple of minutes, until it reaches the consistency of a pouring sauce.

Turn the hot pudding on a platter, remove the paper, cut into squares and pour half the hot sauce over the top.

Secret

- The word sticky comes from the soft middle of this pudding, which is created by the bicarbonate of soda, so do measure accurately to give the perfect middle.

- The sauce can be made up to three days ahead and kept in the fridge.

PLUM AND ORANGE DESSERT CAKE

This creamy, firm cake with fresh plums makes a very tasty dessert served warm with custard or cream. However, it is also perfect enjoyed cold with a cup of coffee. Freezes well.

* Serves 6–8

> 225 g (8 oz) butter, softened
> 225 g (8 oz) caster sugar
> 350 g (12 oz) plain flour
> 3 eggs
> 1 tsp baking powder
> 300 ml (½ pint) double cream
> Finely grated zest of 1 orange
> 8 large plums, quartered and stones removed
> 2 tbsp demerara sugar

You will need a deep, 23 cm (9 in) diameter spring form tin. Line the base with a disc of baking parchment and butter the sides well.

Measure all the ingredients, except the plums and demerara sugar, into a bowl and whisk with a hand-held electric mixer, until combined.

Spoon half the cake mixture into the prepared tin and arrange the plums over the top. Spoon over the remaining cake mixture and level the top. Sprinkle with the demerara sugar.

TWO-OVEN AGA Slide on to the grid shelf on the floor of the roasting oven with the cold sheet on the second set of runners. Bake for 30–35 minutes, until golden brown. Transfer the now hot cold sheet into the simmering oven and sit the cake on top. Continue to cook for a further 15–20 minutes, until well risen and when a skewer is inserted in the centre of the cake it comes out clean.

THREE- AND FOUR-OVEN AGA Slide on to the grid shelf on the floor of the baking oven. Bake for about 30 minutes, until golden brown. Then slide the cold sheet on to the second set of runners and continue to bake for a further 10–15 minutes.

CONVENTIONAL OVEN Bake in a preheated oven (180°C/160°C Fan/Gas 4) for 1¼–1½ hours, until golden brown. If the cake starts becoming too brown, cover it with foil.

Run a palette knife around the edges of the tin and set aside to cool. Remove from the tin, peel off the paper and let the cake cool completely on a cooling rack.

Secret

* If plums aren't available or you would like to ring the changes, this recipe is just as delicious with apricots, apples or pears.

APRICOT AND MARZIPAN DESSERT CAKE

This cake is perfect served cold or warm as a dessert with custard or cream. It is great to make over Christmas time if you have any leftover marzipan. Freezes well.

• Serves 6

> 110 g (4 oz) self-raising flour
> 110 g (4 oz) caster sugar
> 110 g (4 oz) butter, softened
> ½ tsp baking powder
> 2 eggs
> 25 g (1 oz) sultanas, chopped coarsely
> 4 apricots or 1 x 400 g can apricot halves, thickly sliced
> 75 g (3 oz) golden marzipan, coarsely grated
> Icing sugar, for dusting

You will need a deep, 20 cm (8 in) diameter sandwich cake tin or spring form tin. Line the base with a disc of baking parchment and butter the sides well.

Measure all the ingredients, except the apricots and marzipan, into a mixing bowl and beat with a wooden spoon until smooth and combined.

Spoon into the prepared tin and level the top. Scatter the apricots over the cake mixture and press down slightly so they are just covered by it. Sprinkle the grated marzipan over the top.

TWO-, THREE- AND FOUR-OVEN AGA Slide on to the grid shelf on the floor of the roasting oven with the cold sheet on the second set of runners. Bake for about 45 minutes, until well risen, golden brown and shrinking away from the sides of the tin. If it is starting to brown, replace the cold sheet by cooling it down under the tap and returning to the oven or cover it with foil.

CONVENTIONAL OVEN Bake in a preheated oven (180°C/160°C Fan/Gas 4) for 45–50 minutes, until well risen, golden brown and shrinking away from the sides of the tin. If it is starting to brown, cover it with foil.

Set aside to cool, remove from the tin and dust with icing sugar to serve.

Secret

• This cake may look fairly plain, but it tastes delicious. Serve warm with a scoop of crème fraîche on top of each slice to make it extra special. If making ahead and serving warm, sit on a plate and slide into the simmering oven to warm through.

BLUEBERRY CRUMBLE CAKE

This cake is delicious served warm with cream, custard, crème fraîche or ice cream. You can also serve it cold, but I prefer it warm. It's a deep cake, so be sure to use a deep tin. Freezes well.

- Cuts into 6–8 wedges

  300 g (10 oz) self-raising flour
  1 tsp baking powder
  225 g (8 oz) caster sugar
  2 eggs, beaten
  Grated zest of 1 small lemon
  150 g (5 oz) butter, melted
  300 g (10 oz) blueberries

- For the crumble topping

  75 g (3 oz) self-raising flour
  40 g (1½ oz) butter, softened
  75 g (3 oz) demerara sugar
  25 g (1 oz) semolina
  Icing sugar, for dusting

You will need a deep, 20 cm (8 in) diameter spring form or loose-bottomed tin. Line the base with a disc of baking parchment and butter the sides well.

To make the cake, measure the flour, baking powder and caster sugar into a mixing bowl. Stir in the beaten eggs. Add the lemon zest and melted butter and beat again with a wooden spoon until combined.

Spread half the mixture into the base of the tin and scatter over the blueberries. Then spoon the remaining mixture on top and spread until smooth.

To make the crumble topping, mix together all the ingredients in a bowl and crumble with your fingertips to give a fine crumble mixture. Sprinkle over the top of the cake.

Two-, three- and four-oven Aga   Slide on to the grid shelf on the floor of the roasting oven with the cold sheet on the second set of runners. Bake for about 45 minutes, until golden brown. Transfer the now hot cold sheet into the simmering oven and sit the cake on top. Continue to cook for a further hour, or until cooked in the centre.

Conventional oven   Bake in a preheated oven (180°C/160°C Fan/Gas 4) for about 1¼-1½ hours, until golden brown and when the centre is tested with a skewer it comes out clean. Run a palette knife around the edge of the tin to loosen from the tin.

Remove from the tin and remove the paper. Serve warm with a dusting of icing sugar.

Secret

- The cake is just as tasty without the crumble topping, but very special with!

APPLE AND CINNAMON DESSERT CAKE

Apple and cinnamon are a classic, perfect combination for cakes, muffins and tarts. If you are not keen on cinnamon, replace with the finely grated zest of 1 lemon. Freezes well.

- Serves 6

> 175 g (6 oz) self-raising flour
> 175 g (6 oz) caster sugar
> 175 g (6 oz) soft butter, from the fridge (see secret below)
> 1 tsp baking powder
> 3 eggs
> 1 tsp ground cinnamon
> 3 large dessert apples, peeled and cut into fairly thick slices
> 1 heaped tbsp demerara sugar
> Icing sugar, for dusting

You will need a 20 cm (8 in) diameter spring form tin. Line the base with a disc of baking parchment and butter the sides well.

Measure the cake ingredients, except the apples and demerara sugar, into a mixing bowl and beat with a wooden spoon until smooth and combined.

Spoon into the prepared cake tin and level the top. Scatter the apples over the top of the cake mixture. Press down slightly so they are just covered by the cake mixture. Sprinkle with the demerara sugar.

TWO-OVEN AGA Slide on to the grid shelf on the floor of the roasting oven with the cold sheet on the second set of runners. Bake for about 40 minutes, until well risen and golden brown.

THREE- AND FOUR-OVEN AGA Slide on to the grid shelf on the floor of the baking oven. Bake for about 45 minutes, until well risen and golden brown. If getting too brown, slide the cold sheet on to the second set of runners.

CONVENTIONAL OVEN Bake in a preheated oven (180°C/160°C Fan/Gas 4) for about 45 minutes, until well risen, golden brown and shrinking away from the sides of the tin.

Set aside to cool, remove from the tin and dust with icing sugar to serve.

Secret

- You can use fat in a tub instead of butter for this recipe if preferred. Buy one with a high fat content like Stork or Flora Original, not a low fat spread.

NEW YORK VANILLA CHEESECAKE

This is a baked cheesecake, which is very dense and creamy with a genuine vanilla flavour. It can be made up to two days ahead, kept in the fridge and topped with the soured cream to serve. Freezes well.

* Serves 6–8

110 g (4 oz) oat biscuits	25 g (1 oz) plain flour, sieved
50 g (2 oz) butter	2 vanilla pods
1 tbsp demerara sugar	4 eggs, beaten with a fork
900 g (2 lb) full fat curd cheese	150 ml (¼ pint) soured cream
225 g (8 oz) caster sugar	

You will need a deep, 23 cm (9 in) diameter spring form or loose-bottomed tin. Line the base with a disc of baking parchment and butter the sides well.

To make the base, measure the biscuits into a bag and crush with a rolling pin until fine. Melt the butter in a saucepan on the simmering plate (or hob) and stir in the sugar. Add the crushed biscuits and stir so they are coated in the butter and press into the base of the prepared tin (do not push up the sides). Level with the back of a spoon and chill while making the filling.

Measure the curd cheese into a large mixing bowl with the caster sugar and flour. Slice the vanilla pods in half lengthways, scrape out the seeds and add them to the bowl. Whisk with a hand-held electric mixer, until fluffy. Continuing to whisk, gradually add the beaten eggs until smooth. Pour the mixture over the chilled base.

TWO-, THREE- AND FOUR-OVEN AGA Slide the cheesecake on to the grid shelf on the floor of the roasting oven with the cold sheet on the second set of runners. Bake for about 40 minutes, until it is set on top but has a wobble in the middle (if it is still getting too brown on top, you may need to change the cold sheet half way through). Transfer the now hot cold sheet to the centre of the simmering oven and sit the cheesecake on top and bake for a further hour, until set.

CONVENTIONAL OVEN Bake in a preheated oven (180°C/160°C Fan/Gas 4) for 45–50 minutes, until the filling has set. If it starts getting too brown, cover the cheesecake with foil.

Remove from the oven, release the edges with a palette knife, and set aside to cool. Once cool, remove from the tin, transfer to a serving dish and spread with soured cream. Serve cold in wedges.

Secret

* A baked cheesecake always has a dip in the middle – the soured cream is perfect for filling in the gap and gives a lovely sharp contrast to the sweet cheesecake.

LUXURY LEMON BREAD AND BUTTER PUDDING

This is just so delicious. I have used a large amount of custard, which gives a lovely soufflé texture to the pudding and the sugar adds a lovely crispy top. Not suitable for freezing.

- Serves 6

> 8 slices white bread
> 50 g (2 oz) butter, softened
> 4 tbsp good quality lemon curd (or see Luxury Lemon Curd on page 153)
> 300 ml (½ pint) milk
> 300 ml (½ pint) double cream
> 3 eggs
> 50 g (2 oz) caster sugar
> 50 g (2 oz) demerara sugar

You will need a 1.8 litre (3 pint) shallow ovenproof dish.

Butter each slice of bread on one side and then, on top of the butter, spread with lemon curd. Cut each slice into four triangles and arrange them in layers in the ovenproof dish with the points facing upwards.

Measure the milk into a jug, add the cream, eggs and caster sugar and then whisk until smooth. Pour the custard over the bread and sprinkle with the demerara sugar.

TWO-, THREE- AND FOUR-OVEN AGA Slide on to the grid shelf on the floor of the roasting oven. Bake for about 20 minutes, until golden brown and puffed up.

CONVENTIONAL OVEN Bake in a preheated oven (200°C/180°C Fan/Gas 6) for about 25 minutes, until golden brown and puffed up.

Serve warm with a little extra cream if liked.

Secrets

- I have left the crusts on the bread as I like the texture they add.

- Do not overcook the pud otherwise the custard will lose its lovely creamy smooth texture.

- You can use slightly stale bread for this recipe, but it is an old wives' tale that it has to be stale – fresh bread works just as well!

AUTUMN FRUIT CRUMBLE

This crumble is an unusual combination of fruits, but one I think works really well. I like a lot of crumble topping, not a thin layer! Freezes well.

- Serves 6

> 3 large cooking apples, peeled, cored and thickly sliced
> 3 large plums, halved and stones removed and cut into slices
> 3 large peaches, halved and stones removed and cut into slices
> 75 g (3 oz) caster sugar
> For the crumble topping
> 225 g (8 oz) plain flour
> 110 g (4 oz) butter, softened
> 25 g (1 oz) demerara sugar, plus a little extra for sprinkling

You will need a 1.2 litre (2 pint) ovenproof dish.

Arrange the fruit slices in the base of the dish and sprinkle with the caster sugar.

To make the crumble, measure the flour and butter into a mixing bowl and rub together with your fingertips until it becomes like breadcrumbs. Stir in the demerara sugar. Sprinkle the crumble topping over the fruits and level the top. Dust with a little more demerara sugar to give a crisp top.

TWO-, THREE- AND FOUR-OVEN AGA Slide on to the second set of runners in the roasting oven with the cold sheet on the second set of runners. Bake for 30–40 minutes, until golden on top. Transfer the hot cold sheet to the simmering oven and sit the crumble on top. Continue to cook for further 20–30 minutes.

CONVENTIONAL OVEN Bake in a preheated oven (180°C/160°C Fan/Gas 4) for 40–50 minutes, until golden and crisp.

Serve hot with custard.

Secret

- There is no need to cook the fruit ahead, because it has a long cooking time. However, if you are using cooked fruits, just cook in the roasting oven as above – there is no need to transfer to the simmering oven.

Variations

Muesli crumble topping: For a crunchy modern crumble topping, add 110 g (4 oz) of muesli or toasted nuts to the above crumble mixture. Mix all the crumble ingredients together and sprinkle on top of the fruit.

APPLE AND PEAR STRUDEL

This recipe is a variation of the classic apple strudel. Filo pastry can be bought fresh or frozen. If buying frozen, defrost in the fridge as it can get too soft if thawed at room temperature. Freezes well filled and rolled.

- Serves 6

2 dessert apples, peeled, cored and roughly sliced	25 g (1 oz) sultanas
2 pears, peeled, cored and roughly chopped	6 sheets filo pastry
Finely grated zest of ½ lemon and juice of 1 lemon	50 g (2 oz) butter, melted
50 g (2 oz) demerara sugar	25 g (1 oz) fresh white breadcrumbs
	About 110 g (4 oz) icing sugar, sieved

You will need a baking sheet, greased.

To make the filling, put the apples, pears, lemon zest and half the juice, demerara sugar and sultanas into a bowl and mix until combined. Set aside.

Place two sheets of filo, long sides together, side by side on a board or worksurface, slightly overlapping in the middle where they join. Brush with a little of the melted butter. Repeat with another layer, this time overlapping them horizontally. Brush more melted butter over the pastry, and then overlap the final layer vertically, like the first layer. Sprinkle the breadcrumbs over the top sheets.

Spoon the apple and pear filling along the pastry lengthways about 5 cm (2 in) away from the bottom edge and the sides.

Fold the sides in about 5 cm (2 in) and roll the pastry up from the filling end into a sausage shape. Carefully lift the strudel on to the baking sheet and brush all over with melted butter.

Two-, three- and four-oven Aga Bake on the floor of the roasting oven for about 10 minutes, until the base is golden. Slide on to the grid shelf on the floor and bake for a further 20 minutes, until the pastry is golden brown and crisp.

Conventional oven Bake in a preheated oven (190° C/170°F Fan/Gas 5) for 35–40 minutes, until the pastry is golden brown and crisp.

For the icing, mix the remaining lemon juice with as much of the icing sugar as you need to make a thin icing. Drizzle it over the strudel and serve warm with crème fraîche or cream.

Secret

- Strudel is best eaten hot as the pastry will go soggy if left for too long. If this happens or you have frozen and defrosted the strudel, heat it on the floor of the roasting oven (or in the centre of a conventional oven at a moderate heat) for about 10 minutes, until piping hot and the pastry is crisp again.

BLONDE SUET FRUIT PUDDING

This is packed with fruit and the suet makes it sticky and gooey. It is perfect as a light alternative to Christmas pudding. Not suitable for freezing.

• Serves 6–8

3 good tbsp golden syrup
Finely grated zest and juice of ½ lemon
175 g (6 oz) self-raising flour
75 g (3 oz) shredded suet
50 g (2 oz) caster sugar
150 ml (¼ pint) milk
110 g (4 oz) ready-to-eat dried figs, chopped

110 g (4 oz) ready-to-eat dried
  apricots, chopped
110 g (4 oz) ready-to-eat dried
  apples, chopped
1 tsp ground ginger

You will need a 1 litre (1¾ pint) pudding basin. Cover the base with a square of foil or greaseproof paper and butter the sides well.

Mix together the syrup and lemon juice in a cup and pour into the bottom of the basin.

Measure the remaining ingredients into a mixing bowl and beat with a wooden spoon until smooth and evenly combined. Spoon into the basin – the mixture will not fill the bowl, giving it room to rise.

Cut a foil circle about 5 cm (2 in) bigger than the basin, make a pleat in the top and grease the underside with butter. Sit it on top of the basin and seal the edges tightly around the rim so no steam escapes.

Sit the basin in a deep saucepan with a tight fitting lid. Pour boiling water into the pan so it comes half way up the side of the basin. Cover the saucepan with a lid.

Two-, three- and four-oven AGA Bring to the boil on the boiling plate and continue to boil on the simmering plate for about 5 minutes. Transfer to the simmering oven for 3–3¼ hours, until the pudding is firm and nicely risen.

Conventional oven Bring to the boil on the hob and then lower the heat and simmer for about 3 hours, until firm and nicely risen – top up the water if necessary.

Carefully remove the foil and paper and invert the pudding on to a plate. Serve it warm with cream or custard or with Butterscotch Sauce or Luxury Brandy Sauce on page 153.

Secrets

• Suet is easy to buy in shops. It can be found in packets in the baking sections near the flours.

• If making ahead, reheat this pudding in its original pudding basin in the simmering oven (or on a conventional hob, put the basin back into boiling water to steam over a very low heat) just to warm through.

TRADITIONAL CHRISTMAS PUDDING

Whenever I am inventing a recipe I always try to keep the list of ingredients to a minimum without compromising on the taste – but with Christmas pudding there is no getting away from the amount of ingredients needed, but I tried my best! It is important to soak the fruit overnight, so it plumps up and soaks up the alcohol. Can be made up to 3 months ahead and kept in the fridge. Freezes well too.

• Serves 8

75 g (3 oz) currants
50 g (2 oz) raisins
110 g (4 oz) sultanas
110 g (4 oz) ready-to-eat apricots,
  snipped into small pieces
75 g (3 oz) dried dates, snipped
  into small pieces
150 ml (¼ pint) brown ale
1 tbsp brandy
175 g (6 oz) dark muscovado sugar
110 g (4 oz) butter, softened

1 egg
50 g (2 oz) self-raising flour
2 tsp mixed spice
1 tsp ground ginger
1 dessert apple, peeled and
  coarsely grated
Finely grated zest and juice
  of 1 orange
110 g (4 oz) fresh breadcrumbs
50 g (2 oz) chopped almonds
1½ tbsp treacle

You will need a 1.2 litre (2 pint) pudding basin (plastic or china). Cover the base with a square of foil and butter the sides well – this ensures the base does not stick.

Measure all the dried fruit into a bowl. Add the ale and brandy, cover with cling film and leave to soak overnight.

The next day, measure the remaining ingredients into a large mixing bowl, and add the soaked fruits and any soaking liquid. Mix with a wooden spoon until combined. Spoon into the prepared basin. Cover with a lid, or cut a foil circle about 5 cm (2 in) bigger than the basin, make a pleat in the top and grease the underside with butter. Sit it on top of the basin and seal the edges tightly around the rim so no steam escapes.

Sit the basin in a deep saucepan with a tight fitting lid. Pour boiling water into the pan so it comes half way up the side of the basin. Cover the saucepan with a lid.

Two-, three- and four-oven Aga Bring to the boil on the boiling plate and then transfer to the simmering oven for 9–11 hours, until risen and firm to the touch. Test with a skewer to check it is cooked in the middle, if the skewer comes out clean it is. Reconditioned Agas have cooler simmering ovens so it may take even longer.

Conventional oven Bring to the boil on the hob. Lower the heat and simmer for 3–4 hours, until the pudding is firm and nicely risen – top up the water if necessary.

Leave to cool and keep in the fridge until Christmas Day. To reheat, sit the pudding in its basin in the simmering oven (or on a conventional oven, put the basin back into boiling water to steam over a very low heat) for a minimum of 2 hours, to get hot.

Pour over a little more brandy, light with a match, make a wish and enjoy. Serve with Brandy Butter or Brandy Sauce on pages 154 and 153.

Secrets

* If you have run out of time when making the pudding (bearing in mind the cooking time), make it on one day, put into the basin, cover and keep in the fridge and bake the next day when you have more time and all day to check the timings. Like Christmas cake, Christmas pudding should be made well ahead because if it is eaten too fresh, it crumbles when cut – 3 months is ideal, but it can be kept for longer.

* It is traditional to hide a six-penny piece in the pudding and the lucky finder makes a wish. For a change, you can now buy some unusual lucky charms in good cook shops, especially for hiding in Christmas puddings.

CREAMY RICE PUDDING

This is a classic recipe perfect for Sunday lunch as it can be cooking in the simmering oven while you are eating your roast. Not suitable for freezing.

* Serves 4–6

75 g (3 oz) pudding rice	150 ml ($^1/_4$ pint) double cream
40 g ($1^1/_2$ oz) soft light brown sugar	$^1/_2$ tsp vanilla extract
600 ml (1 pint) full fat milk	

You will need a 1 litre ($1^3/_4$ pint) shallow ovenproof dish, greased.

Sprinkle the rice into the prepared dish and cover with the sugar. Mix together the milk, cream and vanilla in a bowl or jug and pour over the rice.

TWO-, THREE- AND FOUR-OVEN AGA Slide on to the grid shelf on the floor of the roasting oven. Bake for 20–25 minutes, until golden brown on top and then carefully transfer to the simmering oven. Leave for about 2 hours, until the rice is completely cooked and the pudding is thick and creamy.

CONVENTIONAL OVEN Bake in a preheated oven (160°C/140°C Fan/Gas 3) for 2–$2^1/_4$ hours, until just golden brown.

Serve warm plain, or with golden or maple syrup if liked.

Secrets

* It may look as though there is a tiny amount of rice in this recipe, but it absorbs the milk.

* You can use 750 ml ($1^1/_4$ pints) semi-skimmed milk instead of full fat milk and cream (but it will only be half as delicious!).

* A tip from my mother – if you are in a hurry, put the rice and milk in a saucepan and bring to the boil, stirring so the rice does not stick – this reduces the cooking time and then you can cook it for just half the time in the simmering (or conventional) oven.

UPSIDE-DOWN PLUM PUDDING

Impressive, easy and delicious – simple as that! Freezes well.

- Serves 6–8

> 110 g (4 oz) butter
> 110 g (4 oz) caster sugar
> 6 plums, halved and stones removed
> 2 eggs
> 175 g (6 oz) self-raising flour
> 1 tsp baking powder
> Finely grated zest of 1 small lemon
> 75 g (3 oz) light soft brown sugar
> 50 g (2 oz) butter

You will need a deep, 20 cm (8 in) diameter cake tin. Line the base with a disc of baking parchment and butter the sides well.

Measure the butter and sugar for the topping into a pan and melt on the simmering plate (or hob), stirring, until just melted. Pour into the prepared tin and lay the plums, cut side down, on top.

Measure all the remaining ingredients into a bowl and beat with a wooden spoon until the mixture becomes smooth, but still fairly stiff. Spoon the mixture over the plums, spreading it out evenly to cover them.

TWO-OVEN AGA Slide on to the lowest set of runners in the roasting oven with the cold sheet on the second set of runners. Bake for about 25 minutes, until just golden brown. Transfer the now hot cold sheet into the simmering oven and sit the tin on top. Continue baking for a further 20 minutes, until set and shrinking away from the edge of the tin.

THREE-, AND FOUR-OVEN AGA Slide on to the lowest set of runners in the baking oven. Bake for 35–40 minutes, until set and shrinking away from the edge of the tin. If getting too brown, slide the cold sheet on to the top set of runners.

CONVENTIONAL OVEN Bake in a preheated oven (180°C/160°C Fan/Gas 4) for 40–45 minutes, until set and shrinking away from the edge of the tin.

Leave to cool for a couple of minutes in the tin. Invert on to a serving plate, remove the paper and serve warm with custard, cream or crème fraîche.

Secret

- It is better to use a fixed-base tin for this recipe rather than a loose-bottomed one to make sure the toffee stays in the tin!

Tarts & Pies

From the classic to the contemporary, tarts and pies are a perennial favourite. Featuring tips on how to make the perfect pastry this chapter provides puddings for everyone and suitable for any occasion.

OPEN TREACLE TART

This is my eldest brother Nick's favourite pudding, so this is for him! Traditionally, treacle tarts have a lattice of pastry on top, but this one is open, just using the short pastry on its base. I also think that some treacle tarts can be too dense with breadcrumbs, but this one is just perfect with its soft centre, which is just as good cold as it is warm. Freezes well.

• Serves 8–10

> 225 g (8 oz) plain flour
> 50 g (2 oz) vegetable lard
> 50 g (2 oz) butter
> 900 g (2 x 450 g cans) golden syrup
> 300 g (10 oz) fresh white breadcrumbs
> Finely grated zest and juice of 4 lemons

You will need a deep, 28 cm (11 in) diameter flan tin.

First make the pastry, measure the flour and both fats into a processor and whiz until like breadcrumbs. Add three to four tablespoons of cold water and whiz again until it forms a ball. You can do this by hand in a bowl if preferred. Roll out the pastry and use to line the tin. Chill while making the filling.

To make the filling, heat the golden syrup in a large pan on the simmering plate (or hob) until runny. Stir in the breadcrumbs, lemon zest and juice and stir until combined and the syrup is runny. If cooking in an Aga pour the filling into the pastry case and level the top.

Two-, three- and four-oven Aga Slide on to the floor of the roasting oven. Bake for 25–25 minutes, until golden brown on top and the pastry is golden and crisp. Watch carefully and if getting too brown, slide the cold sheet on the second set of the runners.

Conventional oven Line the raw pastry case with greaseproof paper and baking beans and bake blind in a preheated oven (180°C/160°C Fan/Gas 4) for about 20 minutes. Remove the beans and paper and return the pastry shell to the oven for a further 10 minutes to dry completely. Remove from the oven. Increase the oven temperature to 200°C/180°C Fan/Gas 6 pour the prepared filling into the case and bake in the oven for about 30 minutes, until golden and firm.

Leave to cool slightly and serve warm or cold.

Secrets

• When lining a pastry case, create a lip around the top – this frames the tart and makes it look very professional.

• If buying a new fluted flan tin, buy one with large flutes, it makes it easier to get the slices out of the tin.

DOUBLE LEMON TART

This is a lemon tart with extra lemon curd, to give it even more flavour. It has a light, fluffy filling that is perfect for serving warm or cold. Freezes well.

- Serves 8–10
- For the pastry

> 225 g (8 oz) plain flour
> 110 g (4 oz) butter
> 25 g (1 oz) caster sugar
> 1 egg, beaten

- For the filling

> 6 eggs
> 600 ml (1 pint) double cream
> Finely grated zest and juice of
>   4 large lemons
> 300 g (10 oz) caster sugar
> 3 tbsp good quality lemon curd
>   (or see Luxury Lemon Curd on p. 153)

You will need a 28 cm (11 in) diameter, loose-bottomed flan tin.

To make the pastry, measure the flour and butter into a processor and whiz until like breadcrumbs. Add the sugar and egg together with two tablespoons of water and whiz again until combined into a ball. You can do this by hand in a bowl if preferred.

Roll out the pastry on a lightly floured worksurface to about 5 cm (2 in) bigger than the tart tin. Line the base and the sides of the tin and prick the base with a fork. Set aside to rest in the fridge while making the filling.

Measure the filling ingredients into a bowl and whisk by hand until smooth.

TWO-, THREE- AND FOUR-OVEN AGA Pour the filling mixture into the tin and slide on to the floor of the roasting oven. Bake for 30–35 minutes, until the filling is set and the pastry is golden brown and crisp. You may need to slide the cold shelf on to the second set of runners after about 20 minutes if getting too brown.

CONVENTIONAL OVEN Line the raw pastry case with greaseproof paper and baking beans and bake blind in a preheated oven (180°C/160°C Fan/Gas 4) for about 25 minutes. Remove the beans and paper and return the pastry shell to the oven for a further 10 minutes to dry completely. Pour the filling mixture into the tin and then return to the oven for 30–35 minutes, until golden and crispy.

Serve warm or cold dusted with icing sugar.

Secrets

- My lemon tart has fewer eggs than other versions, as I like it to be fluffy rather than eggy. For this reason, serve warm, as it could be too runny if cut when piping hot.

- To make ahead, reheat out of the tin on a serving plate in the simmering oven (or low conventional oven) until warm.

APRICOT AND CLEMENTINE FRUIT TART

Here is a delicious crispy pastry base with apricot purée and crunchy streusel topping – the semolina gives a nice crunch on the top. Freezes well cooked.

- Serves 8
- For the pastry

> 225 g (8 oz) plain flour
> 110 g (4 oz) butter, cubed
> 2 tbsp caster sugar
> 1 egg
> Finely grated zest of 2 clementines,
>   plus 2 tbsp juice

- For the crunchy topping
> 75 g (3 oz) self-raising flour

> 75g (3 oz) butter, melted
> 25 g (1 oz) semolina
> 50 g (2 oz) caster sugar

- For the apricot and clementine filling

> 2 x 400 g cans apricot halves,
>   drained
> 1 egg
> 2 tbsp double cream
> 75 g (3 oz) caster sugar

You will need a deep, 28 cm (11 in) diameter fluted flan tin.

To make the pastry, measure the flour and butter into a processor and whiz until like breadcrumbs. Add the sugar, egg, clementine juice (reserving the zest for the filling) and whiz again to form a ball. You can do this by hand in a bowl if preferred. Roll on a floured surface and line the tin. Chill while making the topping and filling.

To make the topping, measure the ingredients into the unwashed processor and whiz to form a ball or beat together by hand. Wrap in cling film and chill while making the filling.

For the filling, wash the processor, add the drained apricots and whiz until smooth. Spoon into a bowl. Add the egg, cream, sugar and reserved clementine zest and whisk by hand until smooth. If cooking in a conentional oven, bake the pastry case as below. Pour into the lined tin and level the top. Coarsely grate the chilled topping so it covers the apricot purée.

TWO-, THREE- AND FOUR-OVEN AGA Slide on to the floor of the roasting oven. Bake for 30–35 minutes, until the pastry and topping are golden and crisp. You may need to slide the cold sheet on to the second set of runners if getting too brown.

CONVENTIONAL OVEN Line the raw pastry case with greaseproof paper and baking beans and bake blind in a preheated oven (180°C/160°C Fan/Gas 4) for about 20 minutes. Remove the beans and paper and return the pastry shell to the oven for a further 10 minutes to dry completely. Continue with the filling and topping as above and then return to the oven for 30–35 minutes, until golden and crispy.

Leave to cool a little and serve warm with cream.

Secrets

- If clementines, satsumas or mandarins are not in season, use orange zest and juice instead.
- It is important to chill the topping otherwise grating will be tricky.

PEAR TARTE TATIN

This classic recipe is usually made with apples, but I have chosen to make it with pears, to ring the changes. Not suitable for freezing.

- Serves 6

175 g (6 oz) plain flour
225 g (8 oz) butter
25 g (1 oz) icing sugar
1 egg

110 g (4 oz) light soft brown sugar
4 just ripe pears, peeled, cored and
    fairly thickly sliced

You will need a 20 cm (8 in) diameter cake tin. Line the base with a disc of baking parchment and butter the sides well.

To make the pastry, measure the flour and half of the butter into a processor and whiz until like breadcrumbs. Add the icing sugar and egg and whiz again until combined into a ball. You can do this by hand in a bowl if preferred. Wrap in cling film and leave to rest in the fridge.

To make the caramel, melt the remaining butter and the light soft brown sugar in a pan on the simmering plate (or hob) and stir until the butter has melted and the two are combined. Pour into the base of the tin.

Arrange the pear slices in a spiral pattern over the caramel in the base of the tin. Continue in layers until all the pears have been used up.

Roll out the pastry on a floured surface to the same size as the cake tin. Lay it on top of the pears and tuck inside the tin edge.

Two-, three- and four-oven Aga Slide on to the grid shelf on the floor of the roasting oven. Bake for about 25 minutes, until bubbling and the pastry is golden brown and cooked.

Conventional oven Bake in a preheated oven (220°C/200°C Fan/Gas 7) for 20–25 minutes, until bubbling and the pastry is golden brown and cooked.

Remove from the oven and allow to cool for about 10 minutes. Then, holding the pastry in place with the palm of your hand, tip the tin and pour the juices into a small saucepan. Boil the juices on the boiling plate (or hob) for a few minutes, until thickened and darker in colour. Invert the tarte tatin on to a serving dish so the pear is on top and pastry underneath and pour the thickened juices over the top.

Serve warm with crème fraîche, cream or ice cream.

Secrets

- It is so important to use a fixed base tin rather than a loose-bottomed one, otherwise the caramel will pour out of the bottom.

- For fun, try this in a 20 cm (8 in) heart-shaped tin – it looks really pretty!

MINCEMEAT, GINGER FRANGIPANE TART

This tart is very special and will feed many guests over Christmas. If time is short, use a bought 500 g (1 lb 2 oz) pack of shortcrust pastry. It freezes well cooked.

- Serves 8–10
- For the ginger pastry

> 225 g (8 oz) plain flour
> 1 tbsp ground ginger
> 50 g (2 oz) caster sugar
> 110 g (4 oz) butter, cubed
> 1 egg

- For the frangipane filling

> 1 x 450 g jar Luxury Mincemeat
> (or see page 42)
> 4 stem ginger bulbs from a jar,
> finely chopped
> 175 g (6 oz) butter, softened
> 175 g (6 oz) caster sugar
> 4 eggs
> 175 g (6 oz) ground almonds
> 1 tsp almond extract
> 1 tbsp flaked almonds

You will need a 28 cm (11 in) flan tin.

To make the pastry, measure the flour, ground ginger, sugar and butter into a processor and whiz until combined. Add the egg and one tablespoon of cold water. Process until the mixture just holds together. You can do this by hand in a bowl if preferred.

Roll the pastry out on a floured surface and use it to line the flan tin. Prick the base of the pastry using a fork. Spread a thin layer of mincemeat over the base and sprinkle over the chopped ginger. Chill whilst making the filling.

To make the frangipane filling, process in the un-washed processor the butter and sugar until creamy, add the eggs and blend. Add the ground almonds and almond extract and process once more. Spoon into the tin and level the top. Sprinkle with flaked almonds.

Two-, three- and four-oven Aga Slide on to the floor of the roasting oven. Bake for 30–35 minutes, until the pastry is golden and firm in the centre. If getting too brown, slide the cold shelf on the second set of runners to prevent the tart getting too brown.

Conventional oven Line the raw pastry case with greaseproof paper and baking beans and bake blind in a preheated oven (180°C/160°C Fan/Gas 4) for about 20 minutes. Remove the beans and paper and return the pastry shell to the oven for a further 10 minutes to dry completely. Continue making the filling as above and return to the oven for 25 minutes, until the frangipane is golden.

Serve warm or cold.

Secret

- Use almond extract rather than almond essence – extract is a natural, true flavour from the nut.

LUXURY MINCEMEAT

I think butter is nicer to use in mincemeat rather than suet as it gives a better flavour and it also means it is suitable for vegetarians. My mincemeat does not contain nuts so is suitable for nut allergy sufferers, too. If you wish to replace the cranberries with chopped almonds, you may do so. Not suitable for freezing but can be made up to 6 months ahead and kept in a cool place.

- Makes 3 x 450 g (1 lb) jars

> 175 g (6 oz) currants
> 175 g (6 oz) raisins
> 175 g (6 oz) sultanas
> 175 g (6 oz) ready-to-eat dried apricots, snipped into raisin-sized pieces
> 50 g (2 oz) dried cranberries, halved
> 1 large dessert apple, peeled and cut into raisin-sized pieces
> 110 g (4 oz) butter, cubed
> 225 g (8 oz) light soft brown sugar
> ½ tsp mixed spice
> ½ tsp cinnamon
> ½ tsp ground nutmeg
> Finely grated zest and juice of 1 orange
> 200 ml (7 fl oz) brandy

Measure all the ingredients except the brandy into a large saucepan. Heat gently on the simmering plate (or hob), stirring until the butter has melted.

TWO-, THREE- AND FOUR-OVEN AGA   Once the butter has melted, cover and transfer to the simmering oven for about 20 minutes.

CONVENTIONAL OVEN   Leave to simmer gently over a low heat, for 10–15 minutes, stirring occasionally.

Let the mincemeat cool, stir in the brandy and spoon into sterilised jars. Seal tightly and label with the contents and date.

Secret

- The butter makes a slightly cloudier mincemeat than using suet, but do not worry as this disappears once the mincemeat is heated or cooked in mince pies or tarts.

MINCEMEAT AND APPLE MINI TARTS

These are a perfect alternative to mince pies, but look much more attractive. Freeze well, but they are also rather good made the day before and reheated on the floor of the roasting oven for 5 minutes to bring back to life.

- Makes 8 mini tarts

> 1 x 375 g packet ready rolled puff pastry
> 1 x 450 g jar Luxury Mincemeat (see left)
> 2 dessert apples, peeled and finely diced
> 25 g (1 oz) golden marzipan, grated
> 25 g (1 oz) chopped almonds
> Icing sugar, for dusting

You will need a baking sheet, greased or lined with non-stick paper.

Lay the pastry on to a floured worksurface and roll to about 2.5 cm (1 in) thick so the pastry is a little thinner. Using a 10 cm (4 in) pastry cutter, cut out eight circles.

Measure the mincemeat, apples and grated marzipan into a bowl and mix together with a spoon. Spoon this mixture on top of the pastry circles, leaving a little gap around the edges so the puff pastry can rise. Sprinkle over the chopped almonds.

TWO-, THREE- AND FOUR-OVEN AGA Arrange the circles on the prepared baking sheet and slide it on to the floor of the roasting oven. Bake for 20–25 minutes, until the sides have risen and the pastry golden brown underneath.

CONVENTIONAL OVEN Bake on the prepared baking sheet, heated first in a preheated oven (200°C/180°C Fan/Gas 6), for 25–30 minutes, until the sides have risen and the pastry is golden brown underneath.

Dust with icing sugar and serve warm with Real Custard, Luxury Brandy Sauce or Malibu Sauce (see pages 153 and 154).

Secret

- You can also use cooking apples for this recipe, but you may need to add a tablespoon of caster sugar to the mixture as cooking apples are sharper than dessert apples.

DOUBLE APPLE GALETTE

This looks so impressive — an apple purée with thinly sliced, glazed apple on top. Freezes well cooked, but better made fresh.

* Serves 6–8

> 4 large Bramley cooking apples
> 50 g (2 oz) caster sugar
> Juice of 1 lemon
> 1 x 375 g packet ready rolled puff pastry
> 3 x pink skinned dessert apples, very thinly sliced
> 4 tbsp apricot jam

You will need a baking sheet, greased or lined with non-stick baking parchment.

Slice each cooking apple in half horizontally (keeping the skin on), then remove the core from each. Arrange cut side down in an ovenproof dish or roasting tin. Sprinkle over the caster sugar and pour over the lemon juice.

TWO-, THREE- AND FOUR-OVEN AGA Bake in the centre of the roasting oven for 10–15 minutes, until the apples are very soft, the skin is lightly coloured and the flesh is coming away from the skin.

CONVENTIONAL OVEN Bake in a preheated oven (180°C/160°C Fan/Gas 4) for 20 minutes, until the apples are very soft, the skin is lightly coloured and the flesh is coming away from the skin.

Set the baked apple aside until easy to handle. Scoop out the flesh of the apple from the skins into a bowl and mash with the juices from the bottom of the dish to make a smooth purée.

Lay the pastry on to a lightly floured worksurface and roll a little large to give a 36 x 26 cm (14 x 10 in) rectangle. Using a sharp knife, carefully score a border 15 mm (¾ in) in from the edge (see secrets, right) and transfer the pastry to the prepared baking sheet. Spread the apple purée inside the border and arrange the sliced apples in three neat rows lengthways over the purée.

TWO-, THREE- AND FOUR-OVEN AGA Slide on to the floor of the roasting oven. Bake for 25–30 minutes, until the pastry is golden and crisp. Watch carefully and if it is getting too dark, slide the cold sheet on the second set of runners.

CONVENTIONAL OVEN Slide the galette off its baking sheet onto a hot baking sheet in a preheated oven (200°C/180°C Fan/Gas 6) for 30–35 minutes.

Meanwhile, put the apricot jam into a pan together with four tablespoons of water and whisk on the simmering plate (or hob) until combined and just hot. When the galette is cooked, use a pastry brush to carefully glaze the top of both the apple and the pastry to give a golden shine.

Serve warm with cream.

Secrets

- When scoring the pastry, make sure you only cut halfway through so it stays attached, otherwise the border will rise separately.

- This is a lovely way to bake apples rather than making a purée from slices of apples — you get the full flavour from the baked skins too.

CUSTARD TART WITH NUTMEG PASTRY

The perfect custard tart must have smooth custard, with no bubbles and crisp golden pastry. Not suitable for freezing.

- Serves 8
- For the nutmeg pastry

  225 g (8 oz) plain flour
  175 g (6 oz) butter
  3 tbsp caster sugar
  1 tsp grated nutmeg
  1 egg, separated

- For the custard filling

  8 egg yolks
  75 g (3 oz) caster sugar
  600 ml (1 pint) double cream
  1 tsp vanilla extract
  Grated nutmeg, for dusting

You will need a deep, 28 cm (11 in) diameter fluted flan tin.

To make the pastry, measure the flour and butter into a processor and whiz until like breadcrumbs. Add the sugar, nutmeg, and egg yolk, together with three tablespoons of cold water and whiz again to form a ball. You can do this by hand in a bowl if preferred. Roll on a floured surface and line the tin. Chill in the fridge while making the filling.

Measure all the custard filling ingredients into a bowl with the reserved egg white from the pastry. Whisk with a hand whisk until smooth. If cooking in a conventional oven, bake the patry case as below. Pour the filling into the pastry case.

TWO-, THREE- AND FOUR-OVEN AGA Slide on to the floor of the roasting oven with the cold sheet on the second set of runners. Bake for 25–30 minutes, until the pastry is golden brown and the custard just set. Sprinkle over a little nutmeg.

CONVENTIONAL OVEN Line the raw pastry case with greaseproof paper and baking beans and bake blind in a preheated oven (180°C/160°C Fan/Gas 4) for about 20 minutes. Remove the beans and paper and return to the oven for a further 10 minutes to dry completely. Reduce the oven temperature to 160°C/140°C Fan/Gas 3. Pour the custard into the pastry case and bake in the oven for 30–35 minutes, until just set.

Set aside to cool, then transfer to the fridge – serve at room temperature.

Secret

- Keep checking the tart during the cooking time. If you have a very hot roasting oven, you may need to replace the cold sheet half way through – do not let the filling bubble otherwise you will have a curdled filling!

FLUTED PLUM TART

This tart looks very pretty and with the added jam has an extra surprise. It can be made and kept in the fridge for up to 2 days and then reheated (see secret, below). Not suitable for freezing.

- Serves 8
- For the pastry

  225 g (8 oz) plain flour
  110 g (4 oz) butter, cubed
  1 tbsp icing sugar
  1 egg

- For the filling

  4 eggs
  110 g (4 oz) caster sugar
  450 ml ($^3/_4$ pint) double cream
  1 tsp vanilla extract
  3–4 tbsp plum, damson or cherry jam
  750 g ($1^1/_2$ lb) plums, halved and
  stones removed

You will need a deep, 28 cm (11 in) diameter fluted flan tin.

To make the pastry, measure the flour and butter into a processor and whiz until like breadcrumbs. Add the icing sugar and egg and two tablespoons of water and whiz again to form a ball. You can do this by hand in a bowl if preferred. Roll on a floured surface and line the tin. Chill while making the filling.

To make the filling, measure the eggs, sugar, cream and vanilla into a bowl and whisk by hand until smooth. Prick the base of the pastry with a fork. If cooking in a conventional oven, bake the pastry case as below. Carefully spread the jam over the raw pastry base. Pour the custard into the tart case.

Slice each plum half into three wedges (leaving the skin on) and arrange on the custard in a neat pattern.

Two-, three- and four-oven Aga Carefully slide the tin on to the floor of the roasting oven. Bake for 35–40 minutes, until the pastry is golden and the filling just set. If getting too brown, slide the cold sheet on the second set of runners.

Conventional oven Line the raw pastry case with greaseproof paper and baking beans and bake blind in a preheated oven (180°C/160°C Fan/Gas 4) for about 20 minutes. Remove the beans and paper and return to the oven for a further 10 minutes to dry completely. Continue as above and then return to the oven for 30–35 minutes, until just set.

Serve warm with a dusting of icing sugar and a little extra cream

Secret

- All custard-based tarts should be served warm rather than hot, otherwise the middle will be too runny. To reheat the tart, slide it into the simmering oven (or low conventional oven) to heat through until warm.

THE VERY BEST BANOFEE PIE

Such a popular dessert and my friend Janey's ultimate favourite. Sometimes the toffee filling can be a little thick and hard but with this recipe, the toffee is just perfectly set and silky – delicious! Not suitable for freezing.

- Serves 8

  250 g (9 oz) oat biscuits
  110 g (4 oz) butter

- For the filling

  75 g (3 oz) butter
  75 g (3 oz) caster sugar
  1 x 397 g can caramel condensed
  3 bananas, thickly sliced
  300 ml (½ pint) double cream,
    whipped
  2 squares of plain chocolate

You will need a 23 cm (9 in) diameter spring form tin. Line the base with a disc of baking parchment and butter the sides well.

To make the base, measure the biscuits into a bag and crush with a rolling pin until fine. Melt the butter in a saucepan on the simmering plate (or hob). Add the crushed biscuits and stir so they are coated in the butter and press into the base of the prepared tin (do not push up the sides). Level with the back of a metal spoon and chill while making the filling.

For the filling, melt the butter and sugar in a large saucepan on the simmering plate (or hob). Add the can of caramel and bring up to a rolling boil for a minute, stirring until smooth. Set aside to cool a little.

Pour on to the biscuit base and spread to an even thickness. Chill in the fridge for 30 minutes to thicken up and set.

Scatter the bananas on top of the caramel and spoon the whipped cream on top, making sure all the banana slices are completely covered. Grate the chocolate on top of the cream. Chill for minimum of 6 hours and serve chilled, cut into slices.

Secret

- Can be made up to 12 hours ahead as long as all the bananas are covered with the cream – if they are in contact with the air they will turn black.

LEMON MERINGUE PIE

This is probably my favourite dessert and one that I would choose for my 'last supper'! Serve warm or cold. Not suitable for freezing.

- Serves 8
- For the pastry

  175 g (6 oz) plain flour
  110 g (4 oz) butter, cubed
  25 g (1 oz) icing sugar
  1 egg, beaten

- For the lemon filling and topping

  Finely grated zest and juice of 4 lemons
  40 g (1½ oz) cornflour, plus 2 tsp
  400 g (14 oz) caster sugar
  4 eggs, separated

You will need a 23 cm (9 in) diameter, loose-bottomed fluted flan tin.

Measure the flour and butter into a processor and whiz together until it looks like breadcrumbs. Add the icing sugar, beaten egg and one tablespoon of cold water and whiz again until combined to a ball. You can do this by hand in a bowl if preferred. Tip on to a floured worksurface and roll out thinly and line the tin. Cover in cling film and chill whilst making the filling.

In a small bowl, mix the lemon zest and juice with the 40 g (1½ oz) of cornflour and stir until a smooth paste. Measure 300 ml (½ pint) of cold water into a small pan and bring to the boil on the boiling plate (or hob). Add the lemon mixture, stir over the heat until thickened and boil for a minute. In a separate bowl, mix together 175 g (6 oz) of the caster sugar and the egg yolks and add to the lemon sauce in the pan. Stir on the simmering plate (or hob) until thickened. Cool for a few moments and then pour into the raw pastry case.

TWO-, THREE- AND FOUR-OVEN AGA Slide on to the floor of the roasting oven with the cold sheet on the second set of runners. Bake for 20 minutes, until the filling is just set.

Measure the egg whites into a large bowl. Whisk on high speed with a hand-held electric mixer, until white and fluffy. Still whisking on maximum speed, gradually add the remaining sugar, a teaspoon at a time, until incorporated and the meringue is stiff and shiny. Add the remaining cornflour and whisk to combine. Spoon over the filling and spread to completely cover the lemon and swirl the top.

TWO-, THREE- AND FOUR-OVEN AGA Slide on to the grid shelf on the floor of the roasting oven with the cold sheet on the second set of runners. Bake for 15 minutes, until the filling is completely set and the meringue is lightly golden and crisp.

CONVENTIONAL OVEN Line the pastry case with greaseproof paper and baking beans and bake blind in a preheated oven (180°C/160°C Fan/Gas 4) for about 20 minutes. Remove the beans and paper and return the pastry to the oven for a further 10 minutes. Continue to make the filling as above. Pour into the tin, top with meringue and bake for 30 minutes.

Secrets

- Always serve a lemon meringue pie warm rather than hot otherwise the lemon filling will be too runny.

DEEP APPLE AND ALMOND PIE

This recipe is like an old-fashioned traditional pie, no fancy edges, just the rustic look. Almond pastry makes it extra special. It can be made a day ahead and reheated to serve. Freezes well cooked.

* Serves 4–6
* For the pastry

>150 g (5 oz) plain flour
>50 g (2 oz) ground almonds
>2 tbsp caster sugar
>110 g (4 oz) butter, cubed
>1 egg, beaten

* For the filling

>1.5 kg (3 lb 5 oz) cooking apples, peeled
>Juice of ½ lemon
>75 g (3 oz) caster sugar
>1 oz (25 g) flaked almonds
>Demerara sugar, for sprinkling

You will need a deep, 20 cm (8 in) diameter, loose-bottomed sandwich tin.

To make the pastry, measure the flour, ground almonds, sugar and butter into a processor and whiz until like breadcrumbs. Add the egg and whiz again until a smooth ball. You can do this by hand in a bowl if preferred.

Roll the pastry on a floured worksurface to about 6 cm (2½ in) wider than the tin. Line the tin with the pastry leaving an over-hang of pastry around the edge. Chill for 15 minutes.

For the filling, coarsely grate the peeled apples and immediately mix with the lemon juice and sugar. Spoon into the pastry case. Fold the over-hanging pieces of pastry so they just cover the edges – there will be a large gap in the middle where you can see apple. Sprinkle the flaked almonds and some demerara sugar over the apple centre.

Two-, three- and four-oven Aga Slide on to the floor of the roasting oven with the cold sheet on the second set of runners. Bake for about 35 minutes golden brown and crisp.

Leave to cool a little (and firm up so easier to slice), remove from the tin and serve warm with cream or custard.

Conventional oven Bake on a hot baking sheet in a preheated oven (190°C/170°C Fan/ Gas 5) for about 50 minutes.

Secret

* The pastry is short and crumbly, so if it breaks when folding over, don't worry – just patch it up, it won't notice!

RHUBARB PIE WITH CRISPY PASTRY

This works so well in the roasting oven of the Aga as long as you cook it on the floor of the oven. It uses short pastry, so it is really crispy. Freezes well.

- Serves 4–6

> 110 g (4 oz) butter, cubed
> 200 g (7 oz) plain flour
> 1 heaped tbsp caster sugar
> 2 eggs, plus 1 egg for glazing, beaten with a touch of milk
> 750 g (1½ lb) young pink rhubarb, cut into 1 cm (½ in) pieces
> 110 g (4 oz) caster sugar
> Demerara sugar, for the topping

You will need a 23 cm (9 in) diameter ovenproof or Pyrex (see secret, below) pie dish.

To make the pastry, measure the butter and flour into a processor and whiz until like breadcrumbs. Add the sugar and 2 eggs and whiz again until combined to form a ball. You can do this by hand in a bowl if preferred. Chill for about 15 minutes.

Roll out just over half the pastry on a floured surface – it should be fairly thin – and use it to line the base of the pie dish. Scatter the base with rhubarb and sprinkle over the caster sugar.

Roll out the remaining pastry and lie it over the top of the rhubarb. Crimp the edges and use any trimmings to decorate the top. Brush with egg wash and sprinkle with demerara sugar.

TWO-, THREE- AND FOUR-OVEN AGA Slide the pie on to the floor of the roasting oven. Bake for about 15 minutes, until golden brown. Slide the cold sheet on the second set of runners and continue to cook for a further 20 minutes, until the pastry is golden underneath and on top.

CONVENTIONAL OVEN Bake on a hot baking sheet in a preheated oven (200°C/180°C Fan/ Gas 6) for 40–45 minutes, until golden brown. If getting too brown, cover the top with foil.

Serve warm with custard.

Secrets

- I have not coated the raw rhubarb in flour as I like the juice from the rhubarb soaking into the sides of the pastry a little, but still allowing the top to be crispy.

- Using a Pyrex pie dish means the juices will not run out of the base and you have the advantage of being able to look underneath to see if the pastry is golden brown.

Variations

Apple and cinnamon pie: Replace the rhubarb with 6 dessert apples, peeled and cut into small pieces. Use a tablespoon of sugar and one teaspoon of cinnamon to scatter over the apples.

Gooseberry and lemon pie: Use the same amount of gooseberries instead of rhubarb. Add the same amount of sugar together with the finely grated zest of one lemon.

Pear and ginger pie: Replace the rhubarb with 4 pears, peeled and cut into small pieces. Use a tablespoon of sugar and one teaspoon of ground ginger to scatter over the pears.

Wicked chocolate

Many people's favourite, no puddings book would be complete
without a chapter full of delectable and luxurious chocolate delights.
Perfect for chocoholics and non-chocoholics alike.

CHOCOLATE BROWNIE CHEESECAKE

This is a rich, dense cheesecake with pieces of chocolate brownie, the perfect way to use up any brownies left in the cake tin. It can be made up to 2 days ahead and kept in the fridge. Freezes well.

- Serves 8

150 g (5 oz) plain chocolate digestive biscuits	150 ml (¼ pint) double cream
50 g (2 oz) butter	3 eggs
110 g (4 oz) 100% Belgian white chocolate	1 tsp vanilla extract
400 g (14 oz) full fat cream cheese	225 g (8 oz) chocolate brownie cake, broken into walnut-sized pieces

You will need a 20 cm (8 in) diameter spring form tin. Line the base with a disc of baking parchment and butter the sides well.

To make the base, measure the biscuits into a bag and crush with a rolling pin until fine. Melt the butter in a saucepan on the simmering plate (or hob). Add the crushed biscuits and stir so they are coated in the butter and press into the base of the prepared tin (do not push up the sides). Level with the back of a spoon and chill while making the filling.

For the filling, break the white chocolate into a heatproof bowl. Sit it on the back of the Aga (or over a pan of simmering water on the hob), until smooth and melted.

Measure the cream cheese, double cream, eggs and vanilla into a bowl and whisk with a hand-held electric mixer or wooden spoon until smooth. Then stir in the melted white chocolate. Stir two-thirds of the brownie cake into the mixture and then pour into the tin. Crumble the remaining brownies over the top.

TWO-, THREE- AND FOUR-OVEN AGA Slide on to the grid shelf on the floor of the roasting oven, with the cold sheet on the second set of runners. Bake for about 15 minutes, until just beginning to set around the edges. Transfer the now hot cold sheet into the simmering oven and sit the cheesecake on top. Bake for a further 40 minutes, until firm around the edges and just set in the centre.

CONVENTIONAL OVEN Bake in a preheated oven (180°C/160°C Fan/Gas 4) for 45–55 minutes.

Remove from the oven, run a knife around the edges and leave to cool in the tin. Remove the tin and the disc of paper and sit on a plate and served chilled.

Secret

- Cheesecakes sometimes crack in the centre when they are cooling. To avoid this, run a knife around the edge while hot, so when the cheesecake cools and shrinks, the edges do not get stuck to the sides of the tin.

CHOCOLATE PROFITEROLES

Profiteroles are such a luxury and a joy to eat. For a change instead of chocolate sauce try Toffee or Butterscotch Sauce page 153. Freeze well filled, un-iced.

- Makes about 14 profiteroles
- For the choux pastry
  - 50 g (2 oz) butter
  - 60 g (2½ oz) plain flour
  - 2 eggs, beaten

- For the filling and icing
  - 300 ml (½ pint) whipping cream, whipped
  - 75 g (3 oz) plain chocolate
  - 5 tbsp double cream

You will need a baking sheet, greased.

To make the choux pastry, measure the butter into a pan, pour in 150 ml (¼ pint) of water and gently bring to the boil (do not boil for longer than 5 seconds otherwise the water will evaporate) on the simmering plate (or hob), until the butter has melted. Remove from the heat, quickly add the flour all at once and beat with a wooden spoon until it forms a ball around the spoon.

Gradually beat in the eggs, a little at a time, to give a smooth, glossy paste. Fit a piping bag with a 1 cm (½ in) nozzle and spoon the mixture into the bag. Pipe 14 balls, evenly spacing them on the baking sheet. If preferred, you can spoon with a dessertspoon, in which case they will look slightly more rustic.

TWO-, THREE- AND FOUR-OVEN AGA Slide on to the lowest set of runners in the roasting oven. Bake for about 15 minutes, until light golden brown and well risen.

CONVENTIONAL OVEN Bake in a preheated oven (220°C/200°C Fan/Gas 7) for 15 minutes.

Set aside to cool a little, and then, once cool enough to handle, make a hole in the side of each profiterole to allow the steam to escape (this prevents them from becoming soggy). Return the profiteroles on the baking sheet to the simmering (or low conventional) oven for about 10 minutes to completely dry out inside.

Spoon the whipped cream into a piping bag and pipe the cream into the hole in the side of the ball. You can also spoon the cream into the centre using a teaspoon if you find this easier.

For the icing, break the chocolate into a heatproof bowl and add the cream. Sit on the back of the Aga (or set over a pan of gently simmering water), stirring occasionally until melted.

Holding the bottom of each ball, dip each one into the icing. Arrange on a tray, chocolate side up, and set aside for the icing to set.

Secret

- If making for a party or buffet, the easiest way to serve the profiteroles is to pile them in a large glass bowl, they can be grabbed and popped in the mouth with no mess.

GOOEY CHOCOLATE PUDDINGS

The posh name for these puddings is 'chocolate fondants' – sponge around the edge with a runny, gooey middle. Make and serve immediately. Not suitable for freezing.

- Serves 8

> 150 g (5 oz) plain chocolate, broken into pieces
>
> 150 g (5 oz) butter, cubed
>
> 4 eggs
>
> 75 g (3 oz) caster sugar
>
> 50 g (2 oz) self-raising flour
>
> 1 tsp cocoa powder, plus extra for dusting

You will need eight size 1 (150 ml/^{1}/$_4$ pint) ramekins, greased and dusted with cocoa powder.

Break the chocolate into a heatproof bowl, add the butter and sit it on the back of the Aga (or over a pan of simmering water on the hob), until melted. Stir and set aside to cool slightly.

Measure the eggs and sugar into a bowl and whisk on maximum speed with a hand-held electric mixer until double in volume, pale and frothy. Sift in the flour and cocoa and carefully fold in the melted chocolate. Fold until evenly combined. Spoon into the prepared ramekins and sit the ramekins on a baking sheet.

TWO-, THREE- AND FOUR-OVEN AGA Slide on to the grid shelf on the floor of the roasting oven. Bake for 9–10 minutes, until well risen, but soft in the centre.

CONVENTIONAL OVEN Bake in a preheated oven (180°C/160°C Fan/Gas 4) for 10 minutes, until well risen, but soft in the centre.

Immediately turn out each pudding on to an individual plate, dust with cocoa powder and serve with crème fraîche. When cut in the centre, the middle should be gooey and ooze lovely chocolatiness!

Secrets

- If you are worried about turning them out as they are hot, just serve in the ramekins with a teaspoon and a spoonful of crème fraîche on top.
- You do need to be accurate with the timings so the middle is gooey – if they are overcooked, they will be like a chocolate sponge, not gooey but still scrummy!

CHOCOLATE AND STRAWBERRY TIER

This looks so attractive and it is so quick to make – it is a fatless sponge, based on a Swiss roll recipe, but I have made it into two tiers instead of rolling it. It is a recipe that I often make in my Aga demonstrations as it is impressive to look at. Freezes well, before cutting or filling.

- Cuts into 8 generous slices

  3 eggs
  75 g (3 oz) caster sugar
  50 g (2 oz) self-raising flour
  25 g (1 oz) cocoa powder
  300 ml (½ pint) double or whipping cream, whipped
  1 tsp vanilla extract
  200 g (7 oz) strawberries, halved
  Icing sugar, for dusting

You will need a small Aga roasting tin or traybake tin measuring 30 x 23 cm (12 x 9 in). Cut a rectangle of non-stick baking parchment just larger than the base and sides of the tin and cut each corner with scissors to the depth of the tin. Grease the tin with butter and then line with the baking parchment, pushing it neatly into the corners to fit.

Measure the eggs and sugar into a bowl and whisk together with a hand-held electric mixer (or use the bowl of a free-standing mixer), until the mixture is light and frothy and has increased in volume (see secrets, right). The mixture falling off the whisk should leave a trail when lifted out of the bowl. Sift in the flour and cocoa, carefully folding in at the same time using a metal spoon. Turn the mixture into the prepared tin, spreading it gently into the corners.

Two-, three- and four-oven Aga Slide on to the grid shelf on the floor of the roasting oven. Bake for about 8 minutes, until golden brown and shrinking away from the sides of the tin.

Conventional oven Bake in a preheated oven (200°C/180°C Fan/Gas 6) for about 10 minutes, until golden brown and shrinking away from the sides of the tin.

Place a piece of non-stick baking parchment a little bigger than the size of the tin on to a worksurface. Invert the cake on to the paper and remove the lining paper. Leave to cool.

Once cold, trim all four edges of the cake with a bread knife to neaten and then cut the cake in half lengthways. Arrange one half on a serving plate. Mix a third of the whipped cream with the vanilla extract and half the strawberries. Spread over the cake on the plate. Sit the other cake half on top. Spread the remaining cream over the top of the cake and arrange the strawberry halves standing upright in even rows on top of the cake.

Dust with icing sugar and, to serve, cut on either side of the row of strawberries to give a sandwich slice.

Secrets

- It is important to whisk the eggs and sugar for a long time so the trail left when the whisk is lifted leaves an impression for about 3 seconds.

- I do not usually sieve flour or cocoa for all-in-one cakes, but it is important for this whisked sponge recipe otherwise the air will be knocked out of the mixture.

RICH CHOCOLATE AND RUM TERRINE

Perfect for any smart occasion, this terrine is rich and luxurious. It can be made up to 2 days ahead and kept in the fridge. Freezes well for up to a month.

- Serves 8–10
    - 175 g (6 oz) plain chocolate
    - 110 g (4 oz) butter, cubed
    - 3 tbsp rum
    - 4 egg yolks
    - 110 g (4 oz) icing sugar
    - 50 g (2 oz) cocoa powder
    - 300 ml (½ pint) double cream, whipped

You will need a 900 g (2 lb) loaf tin, lined with cling film.

Break the chocolate into a heatproof bowl, add the butter and rum and sit it on the back of the Aga (or over a pan of simmering water on the hob), until melted. Stir and set aside to cool a little.

Measure the egg yolks and icing sugar into a large bowl and whisk on maximum speed with a hand-held electric mixer until doubled in volume, frothy and pale, and when the whisk is lifted it leaves a trail. Sieve in the cocoa and carefully fold in. Fold in the cooled chocolate mixture. Finally, fold in the whipped cream to a smooth frothy mixture.

Spoon into the loaf tin, level the top and cover with cling film. Transfer to the fridge to set for a minimum of 6 hours.

To serve, freeze the terrine for about 10 minutes (this makes slicing easier), turn out, remove the cling film and cut into slices.

Serve with mixed summer fruits or Ruby Red Fruit Compote (see page 85).

Secret

- It is important to get as much air as possible into the eggs and sugar – like making a whisked sponge. When folding in the remaining ingredients, take care to carefully cut and fold so as not to knock out the air.

DEVIL WEARS CHOCOLATE

When I invented this recipe I wanted a chocolate cake recipe that is rich, delicious and completely sinful. My brother Mike and I came up with the name after he tasted it! Cake freezes well un-iced.

- Serves 8–10
    - 200 g (7 oz) plain chocolate
    - 225 g (8 oz) butter, cubed
    - 4 eggs
    - 225 g (8 oz) caster sugar
    - 225 g (8 oz) self-raising flour
    - 1 tsp baking powder
    - 1 tsp vanilla extract

- For the sinful icing
    - 200 g (7 oz) plain chocolate
    - 200 ml (7 fl oz) double cream
    - 25 g (1 oz) butter
    - 1 tbsp brandy

You will need a deep, 23 cm (9 in) diameter spring form tin. Line the base with a disc of baking parchment and butter the sides well.

To make the cake break the chocolate into a bowl, add the butter and sit it on the back of the Aga (or over a pan of simmering water on the hob), until melted. Stir and set aside to cool.

Measure the eggs and sugar into a mixing bowl and beat with a wooden spoon or hand-held electric mixer. Add the melted chocolate and butter and stir well. Sieve in the flour and baking powder and stir until combined. Then add the vanilla and mix until smooth. Spoon into the prepared tin and sit the cake tin in a large roasting tin.

TWO-OVEN AGA Slide on to the grid shelf on the floor of the roasting oven with the cold sheet on the second set of runners. Bake for about 40 minutes, until well risen and dark brown. Transfer to the simmering oven for a further hour, or until a skewer comes out clean when pierced in the centre.

THREE- AND FOUR-OVEN AGA Slide on to the grid shelf on the floor of the baking oven. Bake for about 30 minutes. Then slide in the cold sheet and continue to bake for a further $1–1^{1}/_{4}$ hours.

CONVENTIONAL OVEN Bake in a preheated oven (180°C/160°C Fan/Gas 4) for about $1^{1}/_{4}$ hours. If it is getting too brown, cover the top with foil.

To make the icing, measure all the ingredients into a heatproof bowl and sit on the back of the Aga until melted (or over a pan of simmering water on the hob). Stir until smooth and set aside to cool and thicken up to a coating consistency.

Ice the cold cake using a small palette knife to spread the icing down the sides and swirling the top so the cake is completely encased. Allow the icing to set before cutting.

Secret

- This is similar to a brownie recipe so is soft in the centre with a slightly crusty topping.

MOCHA MOUSSE CAKE

This is a recipe I invented by error really, and am thrilled with it! The basic cake is a chocolate roulade, but with a coffee and chocolate filling. It looks stunning cut into slices and is perfect for a smart dinner party. Freezes well, filled and rolled.

- Cuts into 6–8 slices

225 g (8 oz) plain chocolate	2 tbsp brandy
110 g (4 oz) caster sugar	150 ml ($^1/_4$ pint) double cream
4 eggs, separated	1 tbsp coffee dissolved in $1^1/_2$ tbsp boiling water
$1^1/_2$ tbsp cocoa powder	Icing sugar, for dusting

You will need a small Aga roasting tin or traybake tin measuring 30 x 23 cm (12 x 9 in). Cut a rectangle of non-stick baking parchment just larger than the base and sides of the tin and cut each corner with scissors to the depth of the tin. Grease the tin with butter and then line with the baking parchment, pushing it neatly into the corners to fit.

Take two small heatproof bowls and measure 100 g (4 oz) of chocolate into each bowl and leave to sit on the back of the Aga (or over a pan of simmering water on the hob), stirring occasionally until melted. Allow to cool slightly.

Measure the sugar and egg yolks into a bowl and whisk with a hand-held electric mixer on a high speed until light and creamy and full of air. Add one of the bowls of cooled melted chocolate and stir until evenly blended.

In a large mixing bowl, whisk the egg whites with cleaned beaters until stiff, but not dry. Stir a large spoonful of the egg whites into the chocolate mixture, mix gently and then fold in the remaining egg whites. Sieve the cocoa into the mixture and cut and fold until smooth. Turn into the prepared tin and gently level the surface.

TWO-, THREE- AND FOUR-OVEN AGA Slide on to the grid shelf on the floor of the roasting oven, with the cold sheet on the second set of runners. Bake for 15–20 minutes, until risen and shrinking away from the paper.

CONVENTIONAL OVEN Bake in a preheated oven (180°C/160°C Fan/Gas 4) for about 20 minutes, until firm to the touch.

Remove the cake from the oven, leave in the tin and pour the brandy over the cake so it soaks in then set aside to cool. For the filling, whip the cream until it just holds its shape. Stir in the dissolved coffee and then the remaining melted chocolate.

To assemble the cake, lay the sponge flat on a worksurface and trim the edges with a bread knife to neaten. Slice the cake into three even strips lengthways. Put one strip on a plate. Spread half the mocha cream on top, add the second strip and the remaining cream and, finally, the third strip on top. Smooth the filling around the edges and transfer to the fridge to chill for a minimum of 4 hours. Dust with icing sugar and cut into slices to serve.

Secrets

- Be really accurate when cutting the strips. Because they are assembled on top of each other they need to be the same width otherwise the cake will be off-balance.

- Sometimes when melted chocolate is added to really cold cream it can harden a little and set in small pieces. To avoid this, make sure the cream is at room temperature before stirring in the chocolate and coffee mixture and not from the fridge.

LUXURY CHOCOLATE MOUSSE

This is a very grown-up chocolate mousse and perfect for any dinner party. It is quite soft and airy in texture, not firm like some mousses. Please note this recipe contains raw eggs so is not suitable for pregnant women. Not suitable for freezing.

* Serves 8–10

> 75 g (3 oz) caster sugar
> 3 eggs, separated
> 2 tsp cocoa powder
> 100 ml (3½ fl oz) double cream
> 50 g (2 oz) butter, cubed
> 110 g (4 oz) plain chocolate, broken into pieces
> 1 tbsp Grand Marnier
> Icing sugar, for dusting

You will need a large serving bowl or eight to ten glasses or coffee cups.

Measure 25 g (1 oz) of the sugar into a heatproof bowl. Add the egg yolks, cocoa and cream and sit over a pan of simmering water on the simmering plate (or hob). Whisk using a hand whisk until smooth and it will naturally thicken to a thin custard-like consistency. Be very careful not to let the water in the pan boil otherwise the mixture will curdle.

Remove the pan from the heat, keep the bowl over the pan and add the butter and plain chocolate pieces, a little at a time, whisking until melted and fully incorporated. Stir in the Grand Marnier.

Measure the egg whites into a large bowl (or the bowl of a free-standing machine). Whisk on high speed with a hand-held electric mixer (or in the free-standing machine), until white and fluffy, like cloud. Still whisking on maximum speed, gradually add the remaining caster sugar, a teaspoon at a time, until incorporated and the meringue is stiff and shiny and stands upright on the whisk.

Stir a large spoonful of egg white mixture into the chocolate, mix gently and then fold in the remaining egg whites until smooth. Spoon into the serving bowl or individual glasses or coffee cups and chill for minimum of 4 hours or overnight. Decorate with a dusting of icing sugar and serve chilled.

Secret

* You can replace the Grand Marnier with brandy or rum if preferred.

SUMMER CHOCOLATE ROULADE

A popular classic, this one has raspberries added to the cream. For a really impressive dessert to serve many people, make four roulades and arrange end to end on a foil covered long plank of wood – it looks stunning. Freezes well, filled and rolled.

- Cuts into 8 slices

175 g (6 oz) plain chocolate	175 g (6 oz) raspberries
175 g (6 oz) caster sugar	300 ml (½ pint) double cream,
6 eggs, separated	whipped
2 tbsp cocoa powder, sieved	Icing sugar, for dusting

You will need a 33 x 23 cm (13 x 9 in) Swiss roll tin. Cut a rectangle of non-stick baking parchment just larger than the base and sides of the tin and cut each corner with scissors to the depth of the tin. Grease the tin with butter and then line with the baking parchment, pushing it neatly into the corners to fit.

Break the chocolate into a heatproof bowl and sit it on the back of the Aga (or over a pan of simmering water on the hob), until melted. Stir and set aside to cool a little.

Measure the sugar and egg yolks into a bowl and whisk with a hand-held electric mixer on a high speed, until light and creamy. Add the cooled, melted chocolate and stir.

In a large mixing bowl, whisk the egg whites with cleaned beaters, until stiff but not dry. Stir a large spoonful of the egg whites into the chocolate mixture, mix gently and then fold in the remaining egg whites. Finally, fold in the sieved cocoa. Turn into the prepared tin and gently level the surface.

TWO-, THREE- AND FOUR-OVEN AGA Slide on to the grid shelf on the floor of the roasting oven, with the cold sheet on the second set of runners. Bake for 15–20 minutes, until risen and shrinking away from the paper.

CONVENTIONAL OVEN Bake in a preheated oven (180°C/160°C Fan/Gas 4) for about 20 minutes, until firm to the touch.

Remove the cake from the oven, leave in the tin and set aside to cool.

For the filling, fold the raspberries into the whipped cream. Dust a large piece of non-stick baking parchment with icing sugar. Invert the cold roulade on to the paper and peel off the lining paper. Spread the raspberry cream over the cold roulade and, starting from one short edge, roll tightly using the paper to help, and positioning with the join underneath. Don't worry if it cracks – that is quite normal. Dust with icing sugar and cut into slices.

Secret

- Once baked, a roulade was traditionally covered with a damp tea towel and left for several hours, if not overnight, to prevent it from drying out. There is no need to do this – just fill and roll once cold and it will stay moist.

WHITE CHOCOLATE AND BLUEBERRY MOUSSE

Sumptuous and delicious, this mousse will be loved by all. I make it in glasses or glass mousse cups so you can see the ripple effect of the white mousse and purple blueberry purée, which looks so pretty. Not suitable for freezing.

- Serves 6

       200 g (7 oz) 100% Belgian white chocolate
       300 ml (½ pint) double cream
       225 g (8 oz) blueberries
       1 tbsp icing sugar
       1 tbsp lemon juice

You will need six martini or wine glasses.

Break the white chocolate into a heatproof bowl and sit it on the back of the Aga (or over a pan of simmering water on the hob), until melted, stirring occasionally until smooth. Set aside to cool.

Whip the cream to soft peaks. Stir the cooled white chocolate into the whipped cream.

Reserve six blueberries from the measured amount for decorating. Measure the remaining blueberries, icing sugar and lemon juice into a pan and heat for a few minutes on the simmering plate (or hob), until the blueberries start to soften. Whiz in a food processor until smooth. Sieve to give a smooth purée.

Layer the mousse and blueberry purée in the glasses, finishing with mousse on top. Decorate with the reserved blueberries.

Chill for minimum of 2 hours to set and then bring to room temperature before serving.

Secret

- White chocolate can be tricky to melt – use 100% Belgian chocolate and not a high cocoa solid chocolate as these can split too easily. Do not overheat the chocolate otherwise it will appear grainy.

WHITE CHOCOLATE TIAN

This dessert looks smart as it is made in cooking rings so when presented has a perfect spherical shape. Not suitable for freezing.

- Serves 6

    200 g (7 oz) 100% Belgian white chocolate

    110 g (4 oz) white marshmallows

    40 g (1½ oz) butter

    3 tbsp milk

    150 ml (¼ pint) double cream

    6 amaretti biscuits

    Sprigs of mint, to decorate

You will need six 7 cm (2 ¾ in) cooking rings. Arrange on a small baking sheet lined with cling film.

Break the white chocolate into a small heatproof bowl and sit it on the back of the Aga (or over a pan of simmering water on the hob), until melted. Stir and set aside to cool a little.

Measure the marshmallows, butter and milk into a pan on the simmering plate (or hob), stirring until melted. Cool a little, then add the melted white chocolate and stir together.

Whip the double cream and pour the cooled chocolate and marshmallow mixture into the cream, folding well to combine.

Crush the biscuits finely and divide between the bases of the rings, pressing with the back of a teaspoon to form a solid base. Spoon the cream mixture over, levelling the top. Cover with cling film and chill for about 4 hours, until firm or needed.

Bring to room temperature 30 minutes before serving. Sit the rings on individual plates, remove the rings and decorate with sprigs of mint.

Secrets

- Only use white marshmallows, not the pink ones or the dessert will be a strange colour!

- White chocolate and marshmallows are both very sweet, so beware – this is a rich, sweet dessert.

- You can also spoon the mixture into shot glasses instead of the rings if preferred, which will serve more people and give smaller portions.

INDIVIDUAL CHOCOLATE AND HAZELNUT TARTS

These are rich and delicious – and they look pretty, too, with the chopped hazelnuts on top. Depending on your appetite a whole tart may be too large for one person, in which case just cut in half to serve more. Not suitable for freezing.

- Makes 4 tarts
- For the hazelnut pastry
    - 1 tbsp chopped hazelnuts
    - 110 g (4 oz) plain flour
    - 50 g (2 oz) butter, cubed
    - 1 medium egg
    - 1 tbsp icing sugar

- For the chocolate filling
    - 75 g (3 oz) butter
    - 75 g (3 oz) plain chocolate
    - 1½ tbsp golden syrup
    - 2 eggs
    - 75 g (3 oz) light soft brown sugar
    - 2 tbsp full fat crème fraîche
    - 25 g (1 oz) cocoa powder
    - 25 g (1 oz) chopped hazelnuts

You will need four 13 cm (5 in) diameter loose-bottomed tart tins or one four-hole Yorkshire pudding tin.

To make the pastry, whiz the chopped hazelnuts in a food processor until fine. Add the flour and butter and whiz again until like breadcrumbs. Add the egg and icing sugar and whiz to a dough. Turn out on to a floured worksurface and roll with a rolling pin. Line the cases making a little lip around the edge to frame the tarts. Chill while making the filling.

For the filling, melt the butter, chocolate and syrup together in a heatproof bowl on the back of the Aga (or over a pan of simmering water on the hob). Break the eggs into a mixing bowl, add the sugar and crème fraîche and whisk with a hand-held whisk until smooth. Pour in the melted butter and chocolate mixture and whisk again until smooth. Fold in the cocoa and carefully stir until smooth.

Prick the base of the pastry with a fork and then pour the filling evenly between the cases. Sprinkle with the chopped hazelnuts.

TWO-, THREE- AND FOUR-OVEN AGA Slide on to the floor of the roasting oven. Bake for about 10 minutes, until the nuts are starting to turn golden. Slide the cold sheet in on the second set of runners and continue to cook for a further 8–10 minutes, until the pastry is golden and the tarts are just set (they will set completely once cooled).

CONVENTIONAL OVEN Sit the filled tarts on a hot baking sheet in a preheated oven (200°C/180°C Fan/Gas 6) and cook for 20 minutes.

Serve with crème fraîche or a shot of Frangelico or Kahlúa.

Secret

- There is a slightly rippled top to the tarts because the mixture is so gooey – similar to chocolate brownies that ripple on top too.

Express puds

We all lead increasingly busy lives, with less and less time to spend cooking in the kitchen. These recipes are simple and above all quick, but still give impressive results. Ideal for dinner parties where you are pushed for time, or a weeknight when you just want to treat yourself.

ILES FLOTTANTES WITH PASSION FRUIT

This is an ideal recipe for the Aga as the meringues are poached in the simmering oven. Not suitable for freezing.

- Serves 5-6

> 3 eggs, separated
> 175 g (6 oz) caster sugar, plus 1 tbsp caster sugar
> 1 pint (600 ml) milk
> ½ tsp vanilla extract
> 1 heaped tsp cornflour
> 3 passion fruit

You will need a 23–25 cm (9–10 in) shallow ovenproof dish, greased with butter. The dish must have a surface area large enough to accommodate all the meringues.

Measure the egg whites into a large bowl (or the bowl of a free-standing machine). Whisk on high speed with a hand-held electric mixer (or in the free-standing machine), until white and fluffy, like cloud. Still whisking on maximum speed, gradually add the 175 g (6 oz) caster sugar, a teaspoon at a time, until incorporated and the meringue is stiff and shiny.

Bring the milk to just under boiling on the simmering plate (or hob). In a separate bowl, mix the egg yolks, remaining tablespoon of caster sugar, vanilla and cornflour until smooth. Using a balloon whisk, very slowly pour the hot milk on to the egg yolk mixture, whisking all the time until blended. Sieve the custard and return to a pan and heat on the simmering plate (or hob), gently stirring, until the froth disappears and the custard is lightly thickened.

Pour the custard into the prepared dish. Using two tablespoons, make oval shapes from the raw meringue mixture and arrange these on top of the custard – the mixture should make about 10-12 meringues.

TWO-, THREE- AND FOUR-OVEN AGA Slide the dish into the simmering oven. Bake for 15–20 minutes (might be a little longer if you have a converted Aga), until the meringues are soft but just set and no longer sticky when lightly pressed with the finger. The custard will be quite runny still.

CONVENTIONAL OVEN Bake the dish in a preheated oven (160°C/140°C Fan/Gas 3) for 15–20 minutes, until the meringues are soft but just set and no longer sticky.

Cut the passion fruit in half, scoop out the seeds and, using a teaspoon, sprinkle over the warm custard. Serve two meringues per person with the custard while still warm.

Secret

- This dish can be made a few hours ahead of serving and chilled. To serve, cover the dish with cling film and warm in the simmering oven (or very low conventional oven) for about 1 hour.

GLAZED BRIOCHE WITH PINEAPPLE GINGER CREAM

This is perfect for a quick, instant dessert – it is all made in one dish and can be made in 10 minutes. Not suitable for freezing.

- Serves 6
  - 6 slices of brioche from a loaf, about 2.5 cm (1 in) thick
  - 25 g (1 oz) butter, melted
  - 1 tbsp caster sugar
  - 1 x 400 g can pineapple slices, each slice cut into quarters
  - 3 stem ginger bulbs from a jar, finely chopped
  - 250 ml full fat crème fraîche
  - 2 tbsp ginger syrup from a jar
  - 2 tbsp demerara sugar

You will need a 23 cm (11 in) wide based ovenproof dish.

Cut the crusts from each slice of brioche and then brush each side with melted butter and sprinkle with caster sugar. Lay a piece of non-stick baking parchment on the simmering plate (or in a frying pan at a low temperature on the hob) and toast the brioche slices for a few seconds on each side until they turn a light golden brown. Lay in a single layer in the base of the ovenproof dish.

Scatter the pineapple quarters and ginger pieces over the brioche. In a small bowl, mix the crème fraîche with the ginger syrup until smooth. Pour the mixture over the pineapple and sprinkle the demerara sugar over the top.

TWO-, THREE- AND FOUR-OVEN AGA Slide on to the top set of runners in the roasting oven. Bake for 20 minutes, until pale golden in colour and piping hot.

CONVENTIONAL OVEN Bake in a preheated oven (200°C/180°C Fan/Gas 6) for about 25 minutes, until piping hot.

Serve hot straight from the oven.

Secrets

- This does not keep well once baked, and should be made and served immediately. However, the brioche, pineapple and ginger can be assembled up to 8 hours ahead and kept in the fridge. Just pour the crème fraîche and sugar over before cooking.

- Use brioche in a loaf rather than the individual buns for this recipe and cut the slices to give a perfect layer to the bottom of the dish. The remainder of the brioche can be frozen for the next time.

CRÊPES WITH ORANGES AND CARAMEL

So sweet and boozy – simply delicious! Pancakes freeze with no sauce, freeze stacked with cling film or baking parchment between each layer.

- Serves 4

  110 g (4 oz) plain flour

  2 eggs

  150 ml (¼ pint) milk

  2 tbsp Grand Marnier

  3 large oranges, segmented and juice reserved (see secret, below)

  110 g (4 oz) granulated sugar

You will need a 1.5 litre (2½ pint) ovenproof dish, buttered.

To make the pancakes, measure the flour into a bowl. Make a well in the centre, add the eggs and whisk together by hand. Then gradually add the milk, continuing to whisk all the time to give a smooth batter. There are two ways to make pancakes on the Aga.

TWO-, THREE- AND FOUR-OVEN AGA **Method 1** Heat a 20 cm (8 in) non-stick frying pan on the boiling plate and rub around with oil. Spoon in a ladle full of batter and run around the pan so it is even. Cook for a minute or so until the edges curl, flip and cook the other side. Tip on to a plate.

TWO-, THREE- AND FOUR-OVEN AGA **Method 2** Lift the lid on the simmering plate for a few minutes to cool a little, otherwise the pancakes will burn. Rub the plate with a little oil or cover with non-stick paper. Spoon a ladle of batter on to the simmering plate and immediately spread with a palette knife until thin. Once the edges are curling, flip over with a palette knife and cook the other side.

CONVENTIONAL OVEN Make the pancakes in a 20 cm (8 in) non-stick frying pan on the hob, as for method 1, above.

Once all the pancakes are made, roll up and arrange them in the ovenproof dish and keep in the simmering oven (conventional oven set to very low) while making the sauce.

Pour the Grand Marnier and orange juice into a jug and set aside. Measure four tablespoons of water and the sugar into a pan and heat on the simmering plate (or hob), stirring until all the sugar is dissolved. Transfer to the boiling plate (or increase the temperature on the hob) to boil rapidly until caramel colour – do not stir. Pour in the orange juice and Grand Marnier (keeping the pan away from you as it may spit). Return to the heat for a couple of minutes and stir until smooth. Remove from the heat, add the orange segments and then pour over the pancakes and serve warm.

Secret

- Peel the oranges as a whole and remove the segments with a serrated knife, cutting either side of the dividers. With your hands, squeeze the empty shells into a jug to release the juice.

GINGER POACHED PEARS WITH STAR ANISE

Here is my variation on the classic poached pears in wine – I have poached these in ginger beer with stem ginger so they are lovely and gingery. Not suitable for freezing.

- Serves 8

> 110 g (4 oz) caster sugar
> 1 x 500 ml can ginger beer
> 3 star anise
> Finely grated zest and juice of 1 lemon
> 8 under-ripe pears
> 4 stem ginger bulbs from a jar, cut into thin slivers

Measure the sugar, ginger beer, star anise and lemon zest and juice into a wide-based saucepan. Add 600 ml (1 pint) of water.

Carefully peel the pears and cut in half lengthways through the stem. Using a teaspoon, scoop out the core. Arrange the pears, cut side down in the saucepan so they are just covered in a single layer in the poaching liquid.

Bring to the boil on the boiling plate (or hob), and boil for a couple of minutes.

TWO-, THREE- AND FOUR-OVEN AGA Cover and transfer to the simmering oven for 30–40 minutes, until the pears are just tender.

CONVENTIONAL OVEN Cover and simmer over a low heat on the hob for 25–30 minutes, until the pears are just tender.

Using a slotted spoon, spoon the pears into a pretty serving dish and sprinkle the ginger slivers over the top. Reduce the liquid in the pan on the boiling plate (or hob) by a third, so the liquid flavour intensifies and becomes more syrupy. Pour over the pears in the serving dish.

Chill in the fridge until needed (up to 8 hours) and serve at room temperature.

Secrets

- Even though the poaching liquid is reduced, it is still thin and syrupy – don't expect it to be thick.

- Peel the pears smoothly so they are perfectly shaped and make sure you use a wide-based saucepan so the pears lay in a single layer and are therefore covered with the liquid.

BAKED PEACHES WITH ALMOND AND RUM SAUCE

So quick to make and the peaches can then be kept in the fridge, until you are ready to bake them – so there is no need to cook ahead. Not suitable for freezing.

- Serves 4
  4 large white peaches, halved and stones removed
  3 tbsp rum
  50 g (2 oz) ground almonds
  3 tbsp demerara sugar
  10 g (½ oz) butter
  6 tbsp double cream

You will need a shallow ovenproof dish.

Arrange the peach halves cut side up in the ovenproof dish. Pour the rum over the peaches and, using a teaspoon, spoon the ground almonds into the holes where the stones sat. Sprinkle with demerara sugar and top each peach with a knob of butter.

TWO-, THREE- AND FOUR-OVEN AGA Slide on to the top set of runners in the roasting oven. Bake for about 25 minutes, until golden brown and soft, turning the dish round half way through.

CONVENTIONAL OVEN Bake in a preheated oven (200°C/180°C Fan/Gas 6) for about 30 minutes, until golden brown and soft, turning the dish round half way through.

Carefully transfer the peaches using a slotted spoon on to a serving dish. Pour the cream into the bottom of the dish and whisk into the hot rum. Spoon the rum sauce around the peaches on the plate. Serve warm.

Secret

- If you do not want to add cream, you can just spoon the rum sauce from the dish over the peaches when serving, but I prefer it with cream!

MULLED WINE FIGS

This is wonderful at Christmas as the spices are very wintery, but they are also delicious at other times of year, especially in the autumn when figs are in season. Not suitable for freezing.

- Serves 4–6
  8 figs
  150 ml (¼ pint) red wine
  Finely grated zest and juice of 1 orange
  110 g (4 oz) caster sugar
  1 tsp ground mixed spice
  2 cinnamon sticks

Slice each fig into quarters, lengthways, through the stem. Measure all the remaining ingredients into a wide-based pan.

TWO-, THREE- AND FOUR-OVEN AGA Bring to the boil on the boiling plate, add the figs, cover and transfer to the simmering oven for 15–20 minutes, until the figs are just tender.

CONVENTIONAL OVEN Bring to the boil on the hob, add the figs, cover and reduce the heat, leaving the figs to simmer for about 15 minutes, until just tender.

Set aside to become cold, or keep in the fridge for up to 12 hours. Serve at room temperature or warm from the simmering oven.

Secret

- This sauce is very intense and boozy, not a light syrup.

FRUIT PLATTER WITH VIRGIN MOJITO DRESSING

This looks really stunning arranged on a large platter or plate and is a different, more sociable way, of serving fruit salad. If you do not have a platter, use a wooden board or cover a tray in foil and banana or raspberry leaves and arrange the fruits on top. Not suitable for freezing.

- Serves 6–8

    $^1/_2$ watermelon, sliced into quarters and cut into 1 cm ($^1/_2$ in) wedges

    $^1/_2$ galia melon, seeds removed, sliced into quarters and cut into 1 cm ($^1/_2$ in) wedges

    1 mango, peeled and cut into thin strips

    4 passion fruit, cut into quarters

    225 g (8 oz) lychees, peeled

    110 g (4 oz) pomegranate seeds

    For the virgin mojito dressing

    2 tbsp finely chopped fresh mint

    Finely grated zest and juice of 2 limes

    4 tbsp demerara sugar

Arrange the fruits on a large platter in lines or spiral pattern, using one fruit per line. Scatter over the pomegranate seeds.

To make the dressing, mix all the ingredients together in a clean jam jar together with three tablespoons of water, screw on the lid and give it a good shake. Pour some of the dressing over the fruits and serve the rest separately in a bowl to dip the fruits into.

If preparing ahead, cover the platter in cling film and keep in the fridge or in a very cool place for up to 6 hours. The fruits will not discolour and the dressing will infuse into the fruits.

Secrets

- As this is a platter where friends help themselves to a slice or piece of fruit and eat it with their fingers, it is nice to keep the skins on the melons.

- A mojito cocktail is as above but with added white rum.

DRIED FRUIT COMPOTE

This recipe is for my Pa, who loves dried fruit compote at any time of day with a dollop of Greek yoghurt. Not suitable for freezing.

- Serves 4–6

    110 g (4 oz) ready-to-eat dried apricots
    110 g (4 oz) ready-to-eat dried apple
    75 g (3 oz) ready-to-eat dried figs, quartered
    110 g (4 oz) ready-to-eat prunes
    150 ml (¼ pint) orange juice
    75 g (3 oz) granulated sugar
    2 star anise
    1 cinnamon stick

Measure all the ingredients into a pan together with 150 ml (¼ pint) of water. Heat gently on the simmering plate (or hob), stirring continuously until the sugar has dissolved.

TWO-, THREE- AND FOUR-OVEN AGA Bring to the boil on the boiling plate and boil for a couple of minutes. Cover and transfer to the simmering oven for about 15 minutes to soften.

CONVENTIONAL OVEN Bring to the boil on the hob, then cover the pan, reduce the heat and simmer for about 15 minutes to soften.

Pour into a bowl and leave to cool. This compote benefits from being made 12 hours ahead to allow the fruits to soften even more and flavours to infuse. Serve chilled.

Secret

- Sometimes dried figs have a tiny stem in the centre of the base of the fig. Snip this off with scissors before quartering as the stem will never get soft.

RUBY RED FRUIT COMPOTE

This pudding is so quick to make and will be loved by everyone for dessert or even breakfast with natural yoghurt. Not suitable for freezing.

- Serves 4–6

    2 dessert apples, peeled and core removed

    150 g (5 oz) blackberries

    Finely grated zest and juice of 1 orange

    2 heaped tbsp light soft brown sugar

    175 g (6 oz) raspberries

    175 g (6 oz) strawberries, quartered

Slice each apple into very small cubes (size of a hazlenut), put into a saucepan and then add the blackberries, orange zest and juice and sugar. Heat on the simmering plate (or hob), stirring until the sugar has dissolved.

TWO-, THREE- AND FOUR-OVEN AGA Cover and transfer to the simmering oven for about 15 minutes, until the apples are soft.

CONVENTIONAL OVEN Cover and simmer over a low heat on the hob for about 10 minutes, until the apples are just tender.

Add the raspberries and strawberries to the warm compote. Spoon into a bowl and serve cold or warm. If serving warm, this compote is delicious with Brandy Sauce (see page 153).

Secret

- Do not cook the raspberries and strawberries from the start as they will become too soft and break up, but do add to the warm compote so they soften a little.

REFRESHING ELDERFLOWER JELLY

These look so pretty in elegant Martini or wine glasses – perfect for a girlie night or baby shower! They can be made up to 2 days ahead. Not suitable for freezing.

- Serves 6
    - 150 ml (¼ pint) elderflower cordial
    - 450 ml (¾ pint) sparkling water
    - 1 x 11 g packet powdered gelatine

You will need six elegant glasses.

Measure the elderflower cordial and sparkling water into a measuring jug and then remove three tablespoons into a mug. Sprinkle the gelatine into the mug and let the gelatine soak up all the liquid for a few minutes and turn to sponge. Once sponged, sit the mug on the back of the Aga (or in a bowl of boiling water) and leave until the gelatine has dissolved and become liquid.

Pour the liquid in the jug into a pan and very gently heat on the simmering plate (or hob) for a minute (so the liquid and gelatine are the same temperature). Whisk the dissolved gelatine (which is now a smooth liquid) into the pan for 30 seconds – at this stage the mixture will fizz! Immediately pour into the glasses and transfer to the fridge to set overnight.

Serve chilled with a spoonful of Lemon and Lime Sorbet (see page 115) on top.

Secret

- If you have a bottle of sparkling elderflower already mixed in the fridge, use 600 ml (1 pint) of this combination instead of the cordial and water. The flavour will be a little weaker than my version.

CRANACHAN

This is a traditional Scottish recipe and, according to traditionalists, the best way to serve this dessert is to put all the ingredients in bowls and for each person to help themselves to their varying tastes. Mine is assembled in individual glasses or a large glass bowl. Not suitable for freezing.

- Serves 6–8

> 2–3 tbsp porridge oats
> I tbsp light muscovado sugar
> 300 ml (½ pint) double cream
> 300 g (10 oz) raspberries
> 2 tbsp whisky
> 2 tbsp clear honey

You will need six to eight small glasses or shot glasses, or a large glass dish.

Scatter the porridge oats into a non-stick frying pan with the muscovado sugar. Heat gently on the simmering plate (or on hob) until the oats start to colour and slightly caramelise. Set aside to cool.

Whip the cream until it is just softly whipped. Fold in two-thirds of the raspberries and all the whisky and honey, stir to combine. Fold in half of the cooled porridge oats.

Divide the remaining raspberries in the base of the individual glasses or the glass dish. Spoon over the cream mixture and sprinkle each top with the reserved toasted porridge oats.

Serve chilled.

Secret

- For a variation, crush some cooked meringues into the cream.

RACE DAY DESSERT

My gorgeous friend Robbie gave me this idea – she lives near Ascot racecourse, hence the title and it is perfect for a picnic. Freezes well.

- Cuts into at least 12 squares
    225 g (8 oz) butter, softened
    225 g (8 oz) caster sugar
    300 g (10 oz) self-raising flour
    2 tsp baking powder
    4 eggs
    2 tsp vanilla extract
    250 g (9 oz) raspberries
    Icing sugar, for dusting

You will need a small Aga roasting tin or traybake tin measuring 30 x 23 cm (12 x 9 in). Cut a rectangle of non-stick baking parchment just larger than the base and sides of the tin and cut each corner with scissors to the depth of the tin. Grease the tin with butter and then line with the baking parchment, pushing it neatly into the corners to fit.

Measure all the ingredients, except the raspberries and icing sugar, into a bowl and mix together with a hand-held electric whisk until smooth. Pour into the prepared tin. Arrange the raspberries over the cake, in three rows of four clusters, so that when you cut the cake, there will be a mouthful of raspberries on each piece.

TWO-OVEN AGA Slide on to the grid shelf on the floor of the roasting oven with the cold sheet on the second set of runners. Bake for 25–30 minutes, until golden brown and shrinking away from the sides of the tin and springy to the touch.

THREE- AND FOUR-OVEN AGA Slide on to the lowest set of runners in the baking oven. Bake for 25–30 minutes, until golden brown and shrinking away from the sides of the tin and springy to the touch. If getting too brown, slide the cold sheet on to the second set of runners.

CONVENTIONAL OVEN Bake in a preheated oven (180°C/160°C Fan/Gas 4) for about 30 minutes, until golden brown.

Leave to cool in the tin and then dust with icing sugar to serve. Serve cold or warm with White Chocolate Sauce (see page 155).

Secret

- Make sure the butter is soft but not oily. Just allow it to soften in the heat of the kitchen rather than on the back of the Aga, otherwise the cake will be flat.

QUICK RASPBERRY DREAMS

The dark sugar on the top of this completely creamy and delicious pudding melts in a similar way to a crème brulée topping, but without the crunch. Not suitable for freezing.

- Serve 6

> 350 g (12 oz) raspberries
> I x 500 g carton full fat thick Greek yoghurt
> 150 ml (¹/₄ pint) double cream, whipped
> 3 oz (75 g) dark muscovado sugar

You will need six stemmed glasses or a large glass dish.

Take ten raspberries from the weighed amount and mash with a fork in a bowl, so they are squidgy but not puréed. Divide the remaining raspberries equally between the glasses (so they come about a third of the way up the glass) or lay in the bottom of the glass dish.

Spoon the yoghurt into a mixing bowl and fold in the whipped cream and mashed raspberries.

Spoon equal quantities into the glasses on top of the raspberries and level the top. Sprinkle with muscovado sugar and transfer to the fridge for a few hours.

To serve, decorate with sprigs of mint.

Secret

- You do not have to be too accurate weighing the muscovado sugar. This is just a guide, so if you like a thicker crunchier topping, just add a little more.

MA'S RHUBARB FOOL

A fool is a classic recipe, light and creamy with added fruits, and one so familiar to me as my Ma used to make it when we were growing up. Please note this recipe contains raw egg so is not suitable for pregnant women. See below my suggestions for variations. Not suitable for freezing.

• Serves 6

> 450 g (1 lb) poached young rhubarb or 1 x 540 g can cooked rhubarb
> 2 tbsp caster sugar (if using fresh rhubarb)
> 1–2 tbsp icing sugar
> 1 tsp lemon juice
> 300 ml (½ pint) double cream, whipped
> 1 egg white

If using fresh rhubarb, cut it into small pieces, tip into a saucepan, sprinkle over the sugar and add two tablespoons of water.

TWO-, THREE- AND FOUR-OVEN AGA Bring to the boil on the boiling plate and then cover and transfer to the simmering oven for 10–15 minutes, until tender.

CONVENTIONAL OVEN Cook the rhubarb in the pan over a medium heat.

Remove the rhubarb from any cooking juices (or if using canned rhubarb, drain the rhubarb from the tin), reserving the juice, and spoon into a bowl. Mix with the icing sugar (add to taste) and the lemon juice. Fold in the whipped cream.

Whip the egg white until like cloud and fold into the rhubarb cream. Then spoon the fool into a glass bowl or individual glasses. Chill for up to 48 hours.

Secret

• Use any juice from the can or from the poached fruit as extra sauce.

Variations

Apricot: Make the Apricot Coulis on page 155 and fold into the cream and egg white mixture.

Blackberry and blackcurrant: Soften 450 g (1 lb) of blackberries and blackcurrants in a little water and two tablespoons of caster sugar in the simmering oven (or hob) for about 15 minutes, until tender. Mash and fold into the cream mixture.

Gooseberry: Cook 350 g (12 oz) gooseberries in a little water and two tablespoons of caster sugar in the simmering oven (or hob) for about 20 minutes, until soft. Mash with a potato masher and sieve to give a smooth purée. Fold the cold purée into the cream mixture.

Summer fruits: Soften 450 g (1 lb) strawberries, raspberries and blueberries in a little water in a pan on the simmering plate (or hob) for just a few minutes, until they start to soften. Mash with a potato masher. Cool and fold into the cream mixture.

MARSBANA CUSTARD

This recipe is a real cheat and you couldn't find a dessert more wicked or delicious! Children of all ages will love it. Serve it immediately after you've made it. Not suitable for freezing.

- Serves 4

    4 just ripe bananas, thickly sliced on the diagonal

    2 Mars Bars, cut into small chunks

    300 ml (½ pint) custard, bought in a carton (or see Real Custard
        on page 154)

    Ground cinnamon, to sprinkle

You will need a 900 ml (1½ pint) ovenproof dish.

Arrange the bananas snugly in the base of the dish and then dot the Mars Bar chunks over the bananas. Pour the custard over the top and sprinkle with cinnamon.

TWO-, THREE- AND FOUR-OVEN AGA Slide on to the grid shelf on the floor of the roasting oven. Bake for 10–15 minutes, until piping hot (alternatively warm through covered in foil in the simmering oven for about 40 minutes).

CONVENTIONAL OVEN Bake in a preheated oven (200°C/180°C Fan/Gas 6) for about 15 minutes.

Secret

- There's no secret for this recipe – just enjoy it!!

Chilled desserts

Providing an alternative to hot puddings, these recipes are perfectly suited to a warm summer's day or for any time when you want to reduce the time spent slaving away over a hot stove.

BLACKBERRY JELLY TRIFLE

This is a very simple trifle, but slightly unusual as the fruits are set in jelly. If time is short, you can buy a carton of fresh custard from the supermarket. The trifle can be made up to a day ahead. Not suitable for freezing.

- Serves 8

75 ml (3 fl oz) blackcurrant crème de cassis liqueur	2 tsp cornflour
	450 ml (¾ pint) milk
1 x 400 g can pear halves	150 ml (¼ pint) double cream
300 g (10 oz) blackberries	1 tsp vanilla extract
1 x 135 g packet raspberry jelly	1 x packet trifle sponges (8 squares)
5 egg yolks	About 300 ml (½ pint)
25 g (1 oz) caster sugar	double cream, lightly whipped

You will need eight 200 ml (7 fl oz) Kilner jars or glasses or a 2 litre (3½ pint), shallow, wide-based glass dish.

Reserve 8 blackberries from the measured amount for decorating and divide the remaining blackberries between the glass jars or glasses or in the base of the glass dish.

Break the cubes of jelly into a measuring jug and make up to 300 ml (½ pint) with boiling water, stir until the jelly dissolves. Make up to 600 ml (1 pint) with cold water from the tap. Pour the liquid jelly over the blackberries and transfer to the fridge to set for 3–4 hours or overnight.

Measure the cassis into a measuring jug. Then open the can of pears and drain the liquid into the jug so it comes up to 150 ml (¼ pint). Cut the pear halves into small pieces.

To make the custard, measure the yolks, sugar and cornflour into a glass bowl and whisk with a hand whisk until smooth. Measure the milk and cream together in a saucepan. Bring to a scalding point on the simmering plate (or hob) and pour over the egg yolks in the bowl, whisking with a hand whisk until combined. Return the custard to the saucepan and, whisking continuously, bring back up to scalding point until a coating consistency. Add the vanilla extract and pour into a jug and leave to cool.

To make up the trifle, slice each trifle sponge in half lengthways and arrange on top of the set jelly in the dish. Pour over the cassis liquid and leave to soak for about 15 minutes.

Scatter with the pear pieces and then pour the custard over and level the top. Spoon the whipped cream over the custard and decorate with the reserved blackberries. Chill until needed.

Secrets

- If you are making this for children, replace the cassis with four tablespoons of blackcurrant squash and mix with the pear juice.

- Try this different way of serving trifle – in individual Kilner jars it looks so pretty.

APRICOT AND ALMOND GATEAUX

There is no fat in this cake so it is very light and fluffy. This gateau is four thin layers of cake, divided with cream and apricots. Cake freezes well un-filled.

- Serves 8
    - 110 g (4 oz) caster sugar
    - 4 eggs
    - 110 g (4 oz) self-raising flour
    - 50 g (2 oz) ground almonds
    - 1 tsp almond extract

- For the filling and topping
    - 350 g (12 oz) apricots or 1 x 400 g can apricot halves, cut into thin slices
    - 300 ml (½ pint) whipping cream, whipped
    - 25 g (1 oz) flaked almonds
    - Icing sugar, for dusting

You will need two 20 cm (8 in) diameter sandwich tins. Line each base with a disc of baking parchment and butter the sides well.

Measure the sugar and eggs into a large bowl and whisk with a hand-held electric mixer until light and fluffy and when the whisk is lifted it leaves a trail in the mixture.

Sieve the flour into the egg mixture and carefully fold in. Then fold in the ground almonds and almond extract. Spoon into the prepared tins.

Two-oven Aga Slide on to the grid shelf on the floor of the roasting oven, with the cold sheet on the second set of runners. Bake for 15–20 minutes, until golden brown.

Three- and four-oven Aga Slide on to the grid shelf on the floor of the baking oven. Bake for about 20 minutes, watching carefully. If getting too dark, slide the cold sheet on the second set of runners.

Conventional oven Bake in a preheated oven (180°C/160°C Fan/Gas 4) for 20–25 minutes, until golden brown.

Run a knife around the edge of the tins and leave to cool. Turn out on to a cooling rack and remove the paper. Once completely cold, cut each cake in half horizontally using a bread knife, giving you four thin cakes. Fold the apricots into the whipped cream.

Arrange one layer of the cake on a stand, spread with a quarter of the cream mixture and continue layering so the top cake has a thin cream layer on top. Chill, sprinkle with flaked almonds and dust with icing sugar just before serving.

Secret

- If you prefer a lighter filling and topping, use half the amount of cream and 150 ml (¼ pint) of Greek yoghurt mixed together.

AGA BRANDY SNAPS WITH ORANGE CREAM

Brandy snaps can be a little tricky to make as they can burn very easily because of the high sugar content, so keep a careful eye on them. Freeze well layered with kitchen paper in a freezer box.

* Makes 12 brandy snaps

25 g (1 oz) butter	¼ tsp ground ginger
25 g (1 oz) demerara sugar	¼ tsp lemon juice
25 g (1 oz) golden syrup	2 large oranges
25 g (1 oz) plain flour	1 x 200 ml tub full fat crème fraîche

You will need a baking sheet, greased and lined with non-stick baking parchment.

Measure the butter, sugar and syrup into a pan and gently heat on the simmering plate (or hob), stirring until the sugar has dissolved. Set aside to cool slightly.

Sieve the flour and ginger into the mixture and stir well, then add the lemon juice and stir until combined. Spoon teaspoonfuls of the mixture on to the baking sheets about 10 cm (4 in) apart as they spread a lot – you will probably get only about four on a tray, so cook the trays one at a time so, once cooked, you can mould them quickly while they are still hot and before they become cool and hard.

TWO-OVEN AGA Slide on to the grid shelf on the floor of the roasting oven, with the cold sheet on the second set of runners. Bake for 6–8 minutes, until they have spread and are dark golden brown.

THREE- AND FOUR-OVEN AGA Slide on to the grid shelf on the floor of the baking oven for about 8 minutes. If the snaps are getting too brown, slide the cold sheet on to the second set of runners.

CONVENTIONAL OVEN Bake in a preheated oven (160°C/140°C Fan/Gas 3) for about 8 minutes.

Mould the brandy snaps while still warm. For cigar shapes, mould around the handle of an oiled wooden spoon. For round nests, shape around an oiled teacup. For square nest boxes, shape around a small packet of butter wrapped in clingfilm – you can have fun with all sorts of different shapes.

For the filling, peel the oranges and cut out the segments. With your hands, squeeze any juice from the remaining orange shells and stir into the crème fraîche. Mix half the orange segments in with the crème fraîche and spoon into the cold brandy snaps. Decorate each with the remaining orange segments.

Secret

* Instead of crème fraîche you can whip cream and mix with the orange juice if preferred.

CLOUD NINE

This recipe was named by my brother Chris when he was sitting in his garden tasting this recipe. He said that I should call it 'Cloud Nine' because it looks like cloud and you are on cloud nine when you eat it! It is a delicious tropical chilled mousse with fresh fruits and is a variation of a recipe which my lovely hairdresser, Sue, gave me. Not suitable for freezing. Can be made a day ahead.

- Serves 6

    1 x 11 g packet powdered gelatine
    1 x 300 ml carton soured cream
    1 x 400 ml can coconut milk
    75 g (3 oz) caster sugar, plus 2 tsp
    5 tbsp Malibu rum
    1 mango, peeled and sliced
    75 g (3 oz) raspberries
    75 g (3 oz) blueberries

You will need a 1.2 litre (2 pint) glass bowl.

Measure three tablespoons of cold water into a small bowl and sprinkle over the gelatine. Let the gelatine soak up all the liquid for a few minutes and turn to sponge. Once sponged, sit the bowl on the back of the Aga (or in a bowl of boiling water) and leave until the gelatine has dissolved and become liquid.

Measure the soured cream and coconut milk into a bowl. Add 75 g (3 oz) of the caster sugar and three tablespoons of the Malibu and stir until combined. Add a little of the mixture to the dissolved gelatine and mix until smooth. Then pour into the cream mixture and stir until evenly distributed. Immediately pour into the glass bowl.

Transfer to the fridge and leave to set for a minimum of 8 hours, until set or overnight.

For the fruits, mix the mango, raspberries and blueberries with the remaining sugar and Malibu and spoon on top of the set mousse just before serving.

Secrets

- If serving to children and you do not wish to use Malibu, use the same amount of pineapple juice instead. The mousse is a soft set mousse, so do not try to turn it out!

- To get a smooth mousse it is easier to stir a little of the cream mixture in with the gelatine (as explained above) rather than adding the gelatine to the cream mix. I find it works much better.

CLASSIC MERINGUES

Meringues are a wonderful dessert and can be made up to 2 months ahead and wrapped in a bag or box. Freeze well, but they can be easily crushed so freeze in a box.

- Makes about 30 meringues

    4 egg whites
    225 g (8 oz) caster sugar
    150 ml (¼ pint) double cream, whipped
    Raspberries or strawberries, to serve

You will need two baking sheets, greased and lined with non-stick baking parchment.

Measure the egg whites into a large bowl (or the bowl of a free-standing machine). Whisk on high speed with a hand-held electric mixer (or in the free-standing machine), until white and fluffy, like cloud. Still whisking on maximum speed, gradually add the sugar, a teaspoon at a time, until incorporated and the meringue is stiff and shiny and stands upright on the whisk.

Spoon large tablespoons of the meringue mixture on to the prepared baking sheets. You can make them whatever size you like, just make sure they are all the same size so they cook evenly.

TWO-, THREE- AND FOUR-OVEN AGA Slide the baking sheet anywhere in the simmering oven. Bake for about 1 hour 10 minutes, until the meringues are just firm to the touch and can be easily removed from the paper.

CONVENTIONAL OVEN Bake in a preheated oven (140°C/120°C Fan/Gas 1) for about 45 minutes, until they are just firm to the touch and can be easily removed from the paper.

Remove from the paper on to a cooling rack and set aside until cold. Once cold, serve with whipped cream and raspberries, strawberries or other soft fruits.

Secrets

- For a successful meringue, make sure there is no egg yolk in the egg whites otherwise they will not whisk successfully.

- The eggs can be from the fridge, room temperature and a few days old or fresh — it makes no difference!

- If you are using a hand-held electric mixer, be sure to move the whisks around and whisk for a good 10 minutes. A free-standing machine might be a little faster, taking about 8 minutes, as its whisks are slightly larger.

- Do not use a mixing machine with a lid on it — the idea is to get air into the egg whites.

- You must use caster sugar for meringues and not granulated otherwise the meringues will have a speckled top and be grainy to taste.

- Do not add the sugar too soon otherwise the air will be knocked out of the egg whites. Only add it once the whites are as stiff as they can get, and then add gradually while still whisking hard, so the sugar stays suspended in the whites.

RASPBERRY AND LEMON PAVLOVA

Such a classic dessert and one that is synonymous with summer. Use any soft fruits you like. Cooked pavlova keeps for up to 2 months, wrapped in foil in a cool place. Freezes well but be careful as can be damaged easily.

• Serves 6–8

> 3 egg whites
> 175 g (6 oz) caster sugar
> 1 tsp cornflour
> 1 tsp white wine vinegar
> 150 ml (¼ pint) double cream, whipped
> 1 x 200 ml tub half fat crème fraîche
> 3 good tbsp good quality lemon curd (or see Luxury Lemon Curd on page 153)
> 300 g (10 oz) raspberries
> Sprigs of mint, to decorate

You will need a large baking sheet, lined with baking parchment.

To make the pavlova, measure the egg whites into a large bowl (or the bowl of a free-standing machine). Whisk on high speed with a hand-held electric mixer (or in the free-standing machine), until white and fluffy, like cloud. Still whisking on maximum speed, gradually add the sugar, a teaspoon at a time, until incorporated and the meringue is stiff and shiny and stands upright on the whisk. Mix together the cornflour and vinegar in a small cup and stir into the meringue mixture.

Spoon on to a baking sheet in a circle about 23 cm (9 in) in diameter and use a spoon to push up the sides so there is a dip in the middle (like a nest) ready for the filling.

TWO-, THREE- AND FOUR-OVEN AGA Slide into the simmering oven. Bake for about 1½ hours, until a pale cream colour and crispy on top. Set aside to cool completely.

CONVENTIONAL OVEN Bake in a preheated oven (130°C/110°C Fan/Gas ½) for about 1 hour. Then turn off the oven and leave the pavolva in it until stone cold.

Mix together the whipped cream and crème fraîche and stir in the lemon curd and half the raspberries. Spoon into the centre of the pavlova nest. Decorate with the remaining raspberries and mint leaves.

Secrets

• See the secrets on the opposite page for making the perfect meringue.

• The cornflour and vinegar give the gooey middle to a pavlova whereas meringues do not have the cornflour and vinegar and are therefore drier in the middle.

MANGO AND PASSION FRUIT MERINGUE ROULADE

A meringue roulade is much more impressive than serving plain meringues. Mango and passion fruit are my all-time favourite dessert combinations, I would put them in every recipe if I could! Freezes well filled.

- Cuts into 8–10 slices

>   5 egg whites
>   300 g (10 oz) caster sugar
>   2 mangoes, peeled
>   300 ml (½ pint) double cream
>   4 passion fruit, cut in half
>   Icing sugar, for dusting

You will need a 33 x 23 cm (13 x 9 in) Swiss roll tin. Cut a rectangle of non-stick baking parchment just larger than the base and sides of the tin and cut each corner with scissors to the depth of the tin. Grease the tin with butter and then line with the baking parchment, pushing it neatly into the corners to fit.

Measure the egg whites into a large bowl (or the bowl of a free-standing machine). Whisk on high speed with a hand-held electric mixer (or in the free-standing machine), until white and fluffy, like cloud. Still whisking on maximum speed, gradually add the sugar, a teaspoon at a time, until incorporated and the meringue is stiff and shiny and stands upright on the whisk.

Spread the meringue mixture into the prepared tin.

TWO-, THREE- AND FOUR-OVEN AGA Slide the tin on to the grid shelf on the floor of the roasting oven with the cold plain shelf on the second set of runners. Bake for about 10 minutes, until pale golden in colour. Very carefully transfer to the simmering oven and bake the roulade for a further 25 minutes, until firm to touch.

CONVENTIONAL OVEN Bake in a preheated oven (200°C/180°C Fan/Gas 6) for about 8 minutes, until pale golden. Then lower the temperature to 180°C/160°C Fan/Gas 4 and bake the roulade for a further 20–25 minutes, until firm to the touch.

Lay a piece of Bakewell non-stick paper on the worktop and dust with icing sugar. Invert the hot roulade on to the paper, then remove the paper from the base and let it cool.

Cut the mangoes into small pieces (see the secret on page 110) and scoop out the seeds from the passion fruit. Lightly whip the cream, fold in the chopped mango and passion fruit seeds and then spread evenly over the meringue. Starting from one long edge, roll tightly using the paper to help, and positioning with the join underneath. Arrange on a plate, cover with cling film and chill well before serving.

Serve dusted with icing sugar.

Secrets

- See the secrets on page 102 for making the perfect meringue.

- Ripe passion fruit are wrinkly rather than smooth, as you might expect them to be.

- You will find it tricky rolling the roulade without the paper, so make sure it is under the meringue base before you start.

CRANBERRY AND ORANGE SOURED CREAM CHEESECAKE

Here is a softly baked cheesecake with orange and cranberries – light and delicious. Freezes well.

* Serves 8

> 150 g (5 oz) digestive biscuits
> 50 g (2 oz) butter
> 300 g (10 oz) full fat cream cheese
> 150 g (5 oz) caster sugar
> 4 eggs
> 300 ml (½ pint) soured cream
> Grated zest and juice of 1 large orange
> 75 g (3 oz) dried cranberries, coarsely chopped

You will need a 20 cm (8 in) diameter spring form tin. Line the base with a disc of baking parchment and butter the sides well.

To make the base, measure the biscuits into a bag and crush with a rolling pin until fine. Melt the butter in a saucepan on the simmering plate (or hob). Add the crushed biscuits and stir so they are coated in the butter and press into the base of the prepared tin (do not push up the sides). Level with the back of a spoon and chill while making the filling.

For the filling, mix together all the remaining ingredients, except the cranberries, in a bowl and beat with a wooden spoon or spatula until smooth. Spoon into the tin on top of the base and level the top. Sprinkle with the cranberries.

TWO-OVEN AGA Slide on to the grid shelf on the floor of the roasting oven with the cold sheet on the second set of runners. Bake for about 20 minutes, until slightly golden, set around the edges but still with a wobble in the middle. Transfer the now hot cold sheet into the simmering oven and sit the cheesecake on top and continue to bake for a further 30 minutes, until just set.

THREE- AND FOUR-OVEN AGA Slide on to the grid shelf on the floor of the baking oven. Bake for about 45 minutes, until pale golden and set. If it is getting too brown, slide the cold sheet on the second set of runners.

CONVENTIONAL OVEN Bake in a preheated oven (180°C/160°C Fan/Gas 4) for about 50 minutes, until set.

Once removed from the oven, loosen the edges and leave to cool in the tin. Sprinkle with icing sugar and serve cold.

Secret

* Dried cranberries can be found in bags near the nuts and dried fruits in the supermarkets.

QUICK MANGO AND LIME CHEESECAKE

This cheesecake is so quick and easy to make and no gelatine needed! It will be loved by kids and adults alike. Freezes well without the mango topping and glaze.

- Serves 6

  150 g (5 oz) oat biscuits
  75 g (3 oz) butter
  65 g (2½ oz) caster sugar
  1 x 225 g tub full fat cream cheese
  150 ml (¼ pint) double cream
  1 x 200 g tub full fat Greek yoghurt
  Finely grated zest and juice of 1 small lime
  Finely grated zest and juice of 1 lemon
  1 mango
  3 tbsp lime marmalade

You will need a 20 cm (8 in) diameter spring form or loose-bottomed tin. Line the base with a disc of baking parchment and butter the sides well.

To make the base, measure the biscuits into a bag and crush with a rolling pin until fine. Melt the butter in a saucepan on the simmering plate (or hob) and stir in 40 g (1½ oz) of the sugar. Add the crushed biscuits and stir so they are coated in the butter and press into the base of the prepared tin (do not push up the sides). Level with the back of a spoon and chill while making the filling.

Mix together the cream cheese, remaining sugar, cream and yoghurt in a bowl. Add the lime and lemon zest and lemon juice and stir until evenly mixed.

Slice the mango into very thin slices (see the secret on page 110). Cut the mango trimmings and three of the slices (reserve the rest for decorating) into small cubes and stir into the cream mixture. Spoon into the tin, cover with cling film and transfer to the fridge to set for a minimum of 6 hours or overnight.

When set, transfer on to a plate, remove the paper disc (see secret, below) and arrange the mango slices on top in a spiral pattern. Measure the lime marmalade and lime juice into a small pan and heat gently on the simmering plate (or hob). Whisk until smooth and then sieve and use to glaze the mango. Transfer to the fridge until ready to serve.

Secret

- Lining the tin with a disc of paper makes it easier to remove from the tin. Once it is on the serving plate, just pull the paper and it should easily slide from under the cheesecake.

MANDARIN ORANGE CHILLED CHEESECAKE

This is so fresh and light and looks very attractive with the mandarin jelly on top. Can be made 2 days ahead as long as it is kept in the fridge. Not suitable for freezing.

- Serves 6–8

150 g (5 oz) lemon biscuits
50 g (2 oz) butter
5 tsp powdered gelatine
2 x 298 g cans mandarin segments in natural juice
1 x 250 g tub full fat mascarpone cheese

110 g (4 oz) icing sugar
Finely grated zest of 1 orange, plus 3 tbsp of juice
300 ml (½ pint) double cream, lightly whipped

You will need a 20 cm (8 in) diameter spring form tin. Line the base with a disc of baking parchment and butter the sides well.

To make the base, measure the biscuits into a bag and crush with a rolling pin until fine. Melt the butter in a saucepan on the simmering plate (or hob). Add the crushed biscuits and stir so they are coated in the butter and press into the base of the prepared tin (do not push up the sides). Level with the back of a metal spoon and chill while making the filling.

To make the filling, measure three tablespoons of water into a small bowl and sprinkle over three teaspoons of the gelatine. Let the gelatine soak up all the liquid for a few minutes and turn to sponge. Once sponged, sit the bowl on the back of the Aga (or in a bowl of boiling water) and leave until the gelatine has dissolved and become liquid.

Open the cans of mandarin oranges and sit a sieve over a measuring jug to catch the juice, you should have 300 ml (½ pint) in the jug – if you have more, then drink the remainder! Set aside for the topping. Coarsely chop the mandarins.

Measure the mascarpone into a mixing bowl and stir in the icing sugar and orange zest until combined. Stir the orange juice into the dissolved gelatine. Pour the gelatine into the mascapone mixture and stir until smooth. Fold in the whipped cream until smooth. Then add the chopped mandarins. Spoon into the tin and level the top. Chill while making the topping.

Spoon two tablespoons of the reserved mandarin juice from the jug into a bowl and sprinkle over the remaining gelatine. Let the gelatine soak and dissolve as above. Then pour the dissolved gelatine into the remaining juice in the jug and stir. Carefully pour on the top of the filling in the tin and transfer to the fridge to set for minimum of 6 hours.

Remove from the tin, peel off the paper and cut into slices to serve.

Secret

- You must be accurate with the 300 ml (½ pint) of mandarin juice for the jelly topping otherwise the gelatine will not be the correct proportion to set the liquid.

FRUIT SALAD WITH PIMM'S DRESSING

Here is a slightly different fruit salad with a light fresh Pimm's dressing. Not suitable for freezing.

- Serves 6

    2 pink grapefruits, peeled and segmented
    1 large mango, peeled and sliced into thin strips
    1 small cantaloupe melon, peeled and cut into cubes
    ½ small pineapple, peeled and cut into cubes
    2 kiwi fruit, peeled and each sliced into 8 wedges
    3 tbsp Pimm's
    100 ml (3½ fl oz) orange juice from a carton
    2 tsp caster sugar

Prepare the fruit and tip into a bowl. Mix together the Pimm's and orange juice in a mug and pour over the fruit, mixing so all the fruit is coated.

The salad can be made up to 8 hours ahead – serve chilled.

Secret

- Remember that a mango has a flat stone in the middle and so you can't cut it like an avocado. To prepare it cut either side of the flat stone to give two crescent shapes, peel with a small knife and cut up the flesh. You will be left with a flat stone with a little mango flesh around it and you should be able to cut a little more flesh from the stone to add to the fruit salad.

SUMMER PUDDING TERRINE

This pudding is the ultimate summer treat and is delicious served with crème fraîche. I have made this in a loaf tin as I think slices are more attractive, but this recipe will also fit in a 1.2 litre (2 pint) round pudding basin. If you wish to serve fruits alongside the slices, double the fruit mixture. Freezes well.

- Serves 8–10

1 x 11 g packet powdered gelatine
8 slices medium-sliced white
    bread, crusts removed
350 g (12 oz) mixed soft fruits,
    such as blackberries,
    redcurrants and blueberries

150 g (5 oz) caster sugar
150 g (5 oz) raspberries
175 g (6 oz) strawberries, cut into
    quarters
2 tbsp blackcurrant crème de cassis
    liqueur or blackcurrant drink

You will need a 900 g (2 lb) loaf tin, lined with cling film.

Measure three tablespoons of water into a small bowl and sprinkle over the gelatine. Let the gelatine soak up all the liquid for a few minutes and turn to sponge. Once sponged, sit the bowl on the back of the Aga (or in a bowl of boiling water) and leave until the gelatine has dissolved and become liquid.

Place the mixed soft fruits in a saucepan with the sugar and 150 ml (¼ pint) of water.

TWO-, THREE- AND FOUR-OVEN AGA Heat gently on the simmering plate. Stir until the sugar has dissolved, then cover and transfer to the simmering oven for about 15 minutes, until the fruits are just tender.

CONVENTIONAL OVEN Heat gently on the hob. Stir until the sugar has dissolved, then cover, turn down the heat and cook for about 10 minutes, until the fruits are tender.

Stir in the strawberries, raspberries and liqueur. Remove the pan from the heat and leave to cool for a couple of minutes.

Cut the slices of bread so they fit neatly around the sides and ends of the loaf tin, trying not to overlap the slices. Keep a slice or two back to use as a lid. Dip the bread on each side (including the reserved slices for the lid) into the fruit mixture, so the syrup soaks into the bread and turns red. Use the bread to line the loaf tin.

Pour the dissolved gelatine into the warm fruits in the pan and stir. Pour into the loaf tin and sit the reserved bread on top to make a lid. Cover with cling film and leave to set in the fridge for a minimum of 9 hours, preferably overnight. Cut into slices and serve chilled.

Secret

- Older recipes often mention pressing the pudding with a weight. I find this a bit of a hassle hence setting the fruit with jelly, so it is nice and firm and easy to slice.

LEMON SHORTBREAD WITH LEMON CURD AND SUMMER FRUITS

This is perfect for serving large numbers of people and looks stunning too. The cooked shortbread base freezes well.

- Serves 8–10
- For the lemon shortbread
    - 175 g (6 oz) plain flour
    - 75 g (3 oz) icing sugar
    - 175 g (6 oz) butter, cubed
    - 50 g (2 oz) semolina
    - Finely grated zest of 1 lemon

- For the topping
    - 1 x 250 g tub mascarpone cheese
    - 2 tbsp single cream
    - 3 good tbsp good quality lemon curd (or see Luxury Lemon Curd on page 153)
    - 1 tbsp lemon juice
    - 350 g (12 oz) strawberries, hulled and halved through the point
    - 110 g (4 oz) blueberries

To make the lemon shortbread, measure all the ingredients into a processor and whiz until they combine to make a ball. Tip on to a piece of non-stick paper or baking parchment and pat to an even oblong measuring about 30 x 15 cm (12 x 6 in) – it is a soft dough, so easier to pat with your fingers rather than roll with a rolling pin. Prick with a fork and slide the paper on to a baking sheet.

TWO-OVEN AGA Slide on to the grid shelf on the floor of the roasting oven with the cold sheet on the second set of runners. Bake for about 15 minutes, until pale straw colour. Transfer the baking sheet to the simmering oven for a further 20 minutes, until just firm to the touch.

THREE- AND FOUR-OVEN AGA Slide on to the grid shelf on the floor of the baking oven. Bake for about 25 minutes. If getting too brown, slide the cold sheet on to the second set of runners.

CONVENTIONAL OVEN Bake in a preheated oven (180°C/160°C Fan/Gas 4) for 25 minutes, until pale golden in colour.

Trim all four edges of the shortbread while still warm to give neat edges. Set aside to cool completely, then transfer to a serving plate.

For the topping, mix together the mascarpone, cream and lemon curd in a bowl. Stir in the lemon juice and gently spread over the shortbread in an even layer. Arrange the strawberry halves standing up widthways across the shortbread in rows alternating with the blueberries.

Chill until needed but serve at room temperature, cutting slices along the line of fruits using a bread knife.

Secrets

- To make cutting easier, I have made this shortbread mix slightly softer than a classic shortbread biscuit.

- The shortbread can be made up to 2 days ahead, wrapped and kept in a cool place. The dessert can then be assembled up to 6 hours ahead.

BLUEBERRY AND GINGER YOGHURT ICE CREAM

This is a delicious soft ice cream and the blueberries give it a wonderful colour. I like to half stir the blueberry purée in to give a ripple effect.

- Serves 6
- For the blueberry purée

    300 g (10 oz) blueberries

    25 g (1 oz) caster sugar

    1 tbsp ginger syrup from a stem ginger jar

- For the yoghurt ice cream

    4 eggs, separated

    110 g (4 oz) caster sugar

    150 ml (¼ pint) double cream, whipped

    150 ml (¼ pint) natural yoghurt

    4 stem ginger bulbs from a jar, cut into tiny pieces

Measure 110 g (4 oz) of blueberries from the required amount, coarsely chop and set aside.

To make the blueberry purée, tip the remaining blueberries into a pan, add the sugar and ginger syrup and heat on the simmering plate (or hob) for about 5 minutes, stirring until the sugar has dissolved and the blueberries have softened. Cool a little and then tip into a food processor and whiz until smooth.

To make the ice cream, measure the egg whites into a large bowl (or the bowl of a free-standing machine). Whisk on high speed with a hand-held electric mixer (or in the free-standing machine), until white and fluffy, like cloud. Still whisking on maximum speed, gradually add the sugar, a teaspoon at a time, until incorporated and the meringue is stiff and shiny and stands upright on the whisk.

Fold in the whipped cream and yoghurt and carefully mix until combined. Lightly beat the egg yolks and stir into the ice cream mixture and then fold in the reserved chopped blueberries, pieces of stem ginger and blueberry purée. Mix until smooth or leave it slightly rippled.

Pour into a lidded plastic container, cover with the lid and freeze until needed (minimum of 8 hours). Remove from the freezer about 10 minutes before serving to make scooping easier.

Secret

- This is quite a 'grown up' ice cream and perfect for serving in the summer after a supper party. Kids love it too, but if they are not keen on ginger, just leave it out and replace the ginger syrup in the purée with another 25 g (1 oz) of caster sugar.

LEMON AND LIME SORBET

Sorbet is so refreshing on warm summer days. Keep in the freezer for up to a month.

- Serves 6–8
    450 g (1 lb) caster sugar
    Finely grated zest and juice of 2 lemons
    Finely grated zest and juice of 4 limes

Measure the sugar and lemon and lime zest into a pan together with 150 ml (¼ pint) of water. Heat on the simmering plate (or hob), stirring all the time, until the sugar has completely dissolved. Remove the spoon from the pan and boil rapidly until the syrup has reduced by half and is quite tacky.

Add the lemon and lime juice and a further 600 ml (1 pint) of water and stir. Set aside to cool. Pour into a lidded plastic container and cover with the lid.

Freeze overnight or until icy like snow, then whiz in the food processor until creamy and smooth. Re-freeze for a minimum of 1 hour or keep in the freezer until ready to use. Remove from the freezer about 15 minutes before serving to make scooping easier.

Secrets

- Before whizzing to become smooth, break up the sorbet with a little knife.

- Whiz until there are no lumps and the sorbet is completely smooth.

Variations

Blackcurrant sorbet: Use 450 g (1 lb) blackcurrants and the zest and juice of 1 lemon. Omit the limes. Cook the blackcurrants in the simmering oven (or very low conventional oven) until tender. Whiz in the processor until smooth and transfer to a heatproof bowl. Pour the syrup on to the blackcurrant purée and continue as above.

Mango and lime sorbet: Use 2 large mangoes, peeled and cut into pieces and the grated zest and juice of 4 limes. Omit the lemons. Whiz the mango flesh in a processor until smooth and transfer to a heatproof bowl. Pour the syrup on to the mango purée and continue as above.

Peach sorbet: Use 10 peaches and the finely grated zest and juice of 2 lemons. Omit the limes. Remove the skin from the peaches either by peeling with a knife or by plunging into boiling water for about 6 seconds. Remove from the water with a slotted spoon and the skin will peel easily. Cut into quarters, remove the stone and discard and put the flesh into a food processor. Whiz until smooth and transfer to a heatproof bowl. Pour the syrup on to the peach purée and continue as above.

Raspberry sorbet: Use 450 g (1 lb) raspberries and the zest and juice of 1 lemon. Omit the limes. Whiz until smooth and transfer to a heatproof bowl. Pour the syrup on to the raspberry purée and continue as above.

Strawberry sorbet: Make as for the raspberry sorbet.

VANILLA AND BLACKBERRY ICED PARFAIT

This is a great dessert. It looks impressive and can be kept in the freezer for up to a month.

- Cuts into 8–10 thin slices

> 450 g (1 lb) blackberries or blackcurrants
> 110 g (4 oz) caster sugar
> 2 tbsp blackcurrant crème de cassis liqueur
> 150 ml (¼ pint) double cream
> 600 ml (1 pint) ready-made fresh vanilla custard (or see Real Custard on page 154)
> 6 trifle sponges, each sliced in half horizontally

You will need a 900 g (2 lb) loaf tin, lined with cling film.

Measure the blackberries and sugar into a pan.

TWO-, THREE- AND FOUR-OVEN AGA Heat gently on the simmering plate, stirring, for about 2 minutes. Cover and transfer to the simmering oven for about 15 minutes, until soft.

CONVENTIONAL OVEN Heat gently on the hob for about 15 minutes, until soft.

Add the cassis and transfer to the fridge to chill.

Whisk the double cream to soft peaks and then add the custard and mix until smooth. Spoon the cream mixture into the lined tin and level the top. Carefully spoon half of the cold blackberry compote over the custard (a little of the juice will ooze into the custard).

Arrange a single layer of trifle sponges over the fruit (you may need to trim the sponge to fit neatly) and then gently press the sponge into the compote so the sponges are level with the top of the tin and soak up the juices. Cover with cling film and freeze overnight or until ready to serve.

To serve, remove the parfait from the freezer for 1–2 hours before eating. The parfait should be half frozen but easy to slice. Warm the remaining compote and serve over the top of each slice.

Secrets

- If you are making the parfait well in advance, you can freeze the remaining compote in a separate container and then defrost in the fridge to serve.

- If you have parfait left over, you can re-freeze if you do so immediately, or it is just as delicious completely thawed and soft, but keep in the fridge.

Little pots & glasses

Served in anything from an elegant long-stemmed glass to a pretty ramekin these delightful desserts look wonderful and you can have lots of fun in how you choose to serve them. Indulgent desserts in small sizes they are perfect for dinner with friends or when you fancy a small luxury.

TOTALLY DIVINE PLUM AND CUSTARD POTS

These are to die for! Plum with lightly set custard ... I have made them in ramekins as they look lovely served individually. Once baked, they will happily keep warm for about 30 minutes in the simmering oven or low oven. Not suitable for freezing.

- Serves 8
    A knob of butter
    4 plums, halved and stones removed, and then cut into large pieces
    4 eggs
    175 g (6 oz) caster sugar
    300 ml (½ pint) double cream
    ½ tsp vanilla extract
    2 tbsp demerara sugar

You will need eight size 1 (150 ml/¼ pint) ramekins, lightly buttered.

Melt the butter in a saucepan and add the cut plums.

TWO-, THREE- AND FOUR-OVEN AGA Heat on the boiling plate for a minute and then cover and transfer to the simmering oven for 5–10 minutes, until just soft but still in pieces and not mush.

CONVENTIONAL OVEN Soften the plums on the hob for about 8 minutes.

Meanwhile, to make the custard, break the eggs into a mixing bowl and add the sugar. Beat with a small whisk until well combined (no need to add any air). Then add the cream and vanilla and whisk again until thoroughly combined.

Divide the plums evenly among the ramekins. Pour the custard into a jug and pour over the plums and then sprinkle with demerara sugar. Sit the ramekins on a baking sheet.

TWO-OVEN AGA Slide on to the second set of runners in the roasting oven. Bake for about 12 minutes, until golden brown, set like sponge around the edge but still soft in the middle.

THREE- AND FOUR-OVEN AGA Slide on to the second set of runners in the baking oven. Bake for about 15 minutes, until golden brown, set like sponge around the edge but still soft in the middle.

CONVENTIONAL OVEN Bake the ramekins in a preheated oven (200°C/180°C Fan/Gas 6) for 12–15 minutes.

Set aside to cool for about 5 minutes, but serve warm.

Secret

- The centre of the pot should be like thick custard, so be careful not to overcook.

RHUBARB CUSTARD MERINGUE TREAT

These are so quick to make and a great combination of flavours. It is the perfect recipe for using leftover meringues or make some (see page 102), or, for a real cheat, buy some from your supermarket. Not suitable for freezing.

- Serves 6
  > 300 g (10 oz) young pink rhubarb
  > 25 g (1 oz) caster sugar
  > 75 g (3 oz) meringues, coarsely crushed
  > 300 ml (½ pint) Real Custard (see page 154)
  > 1 x 200 g tub full fat Greek yoghurt

You will need six glasses or a large glass bowl.

Cut the rhubarb into small pieces, tip into a saucepan, sprinkle over the sugar and add two tablespoons of water.

TWO-, THREE- AND FOUR-OVEN AGA Bring to the boil on the boiling plate and then cover and transfer to the simmering oven for 10–15 minutes, until tender.

CONVENTIONAL OVEN Cook the rhubarb in the pan over a medium heat.

Set aside to cool completely.

Sprinkle half the crushed meringue into the base of the glasses or glass bowl. Measure the custard and yoghurt into a mixing bowl and stir together until smooth. Spoon half the custard into the glasses on top of the meringues and then spoon half the rhubarb on to the custard. Repeat the layers again so you finish with the meringue on the top.

Chill in the fridge up to 1 hour before serving (or can be made up to 6 hours ahead).

Secrets

- See the secrets on page 102 for making the perfect meringue.
- When breaking up the meringues, keep the pieces quite chunky, especially if making ahead as they will soften from the moisture of the custard and you want to keep a crunch.
- It is prettier to use fresh rhubarb as the bright pink colour looks lovely. If making out of the rhubarb season, use a 560 g can of cooked rhubarb, drained well.

Variations

- Replace the rhubarb with an equal quantity of other soft cooked fruits, if liked, such as raspberries, blackberries, blackcurrants, gooseberries or redcurrants.

STICKY PEAR DELIGHT

These are similar to a toffee pudding, but are much quicker to make. Not suitable for freezing.

- Serves 6

> 110 g (4 oz) butter
> 110 g (4 oz) golden syrup
> 5 tbsp double cream
> 4 pears, peeled and roughly chopped
> 175 g (6 oz) all-butter shortbread biscuits, finely crushed

You will need six size 1 (150 ml/¼ pint) ramekins.

Measure the butter, syrup and cream into a small pan and melt on the simmering plate (or hob), until smooth.

Pour half the sauce into the bases of the ramekins, divided evenly. Arrange half of the pears on top of the sauce and then sprinkle half of the crushed biscuits on top of the pear. Top with the remaining pear pieces, then the remaining biscuits and finally pour over the remaining sauce. Arrange the ramekins on a baking sheet.

TWO-, THREE- AND FOUR-OVEN AGA Slide the baking sheet on to the second set of runners in the roasting tin. Bake for about 15 minutes, until golden and bubbling.

CONVENTIONAL OVEN Bake in a preheated oven (190°C/170°C Fan/Gas 5) for 15–20 minutes, until golden and bubbling.

Serve warm with a spoonful of vanilla ice cream on top.

Secret

- This dessert is very rich, hence using small ramekins. I think it would be too rich served in a large dish as the serving spoonfuls may be too large!

TIRAMISU AND STRAWBERRY MOUSSE

This tiramisu is similar to the classic Italian dessert, but it is quicker to make and is more like a mousse. With a layer of strawberries, the pudding looks lovely in tall glasses. You can always make it layered in a large dish if you prefer. Not suitable for freezing.

* Serves 8

> 150 ml (¼ pint) boiling water
> 1 tbsp instant coffee granules
> 2 tbsp brandy
> 16 sponge fingers
> 1 x 500 g tub mascarpone
> 1 x 375 g can condensed milk
> 225 g (8 oz) strawberries, thinly sliced
> 50 g (2 oz) plain chocolate, coarsely chopped

You will need eight tall-stemmed wine glasses or 12 smaller shot glasses.

Measure the boiling water from a kettle on the boiling plate of the Aga (or an electric kettle) into a jug. Then measure the coffee into a shallow heatproof dish and pour over the boiling water and brandy and mix until the coffee is dissolved. Add the sponge fingers and leave to absorb the liquid.

Measure the mascarpone and condensed milk into a bowl and, using a hand-held electric mixer (or free-standing mixer) whisk for a few minutes, until thick and mousse-like.

Arrange the soaked sponge fingers in the base of eight tall-stemmed wine glasses or 12 smaller shot glasses, sharing them equally. Then arrange the sliced strawberries over the top and spoon in the mascarpone mousse. Sprinkle the chopped chocolate over the top.

Chill until firm and serve from the fridge.

Secret

* Do not over whisk the mascarpone and condensed milk otherwise it will be too thick, just whisk until like a cloud – light and fluffy and holds its shape.

* If you omit the strawberries and just make this as a tiramisu, then it will freeze.

DIVINE CHOCOLATE AND PEPPERMINT MOUSSE

On holiday in France last year I had a wonderful mint and chocolate mousse – two layers of chocolate with a fluffy mint topping. It was truly divine and from the first taste I vowed to try to re-create the recipe (the chef in the restaurant would not divulge it!), so here is my version. It looks stunning made in little glass pots, but is very rich so serve in small pots with a teaspoon. Not suitable for freezing.

- Serves 8–10
      150 g (5 oz) plain chocolate, broken into pieces, plus a little extra for grating
      300 ml (½ pint) double cream
      150 g (5 oz) milk chocolate, broken into pieces
      1 egg white
      2 tsp peppermint extract
      Sprigs of fresh mint, to garnish (optional)

First make the chocolate layers. Break the plain chocolate and 150 ml (¼ pint) of the cream into a heatproof bowl. Break the milk chocolate into a separate heatproof bowl.

TWO-, THREE- AND FOUR-OVEN AGA Sit both bowls on the back of the Aga, stirring occasionally until the chocolate has melted.

CONVENTIONAL OVEN Melt the chocolate in each bowl over a pan of just simmering water, stirring occasionally until it has melted.

Set the bowls aside to cool slightly. Once the milk chocolate is just cool, stir in 60 ml (2 fl oz) of the remaining double cream until smooth.

Spoon the milk chocolate mixture into the base of eight small glass pots or one large glass bowl – it should come to about a third of the way up the pot. Spoon over the plain chocolate to give another, thinner, chocolate layer – these two layers should sit in a line, do not mix together. Transfer to the fridge to firm up while making the topping.

Whisk the egg white until like a cloud, using a hand-held electric mixer. Wash the beaters and then whisk the remaining double cream in a separate bowl, until lightly whipped. Mix the egg white with the whipped cream, carefully folding so they both stay light and fluffy. Fold in the peppermint extract.

Spoon the peppermint cream on top of each pot and transfer to the fridge to set. This pudding is best made on the day, but take it out of the fridge 30 minutes before serving otherwise the chocolate layers will be a little too firm to eat. Finely grate extra chocolate and garnish with a sprig of mint to serve.

Secret

- Use a plain chocolate with about 39% cocoa solids rather than a posh chocolate with over 70% cocoa solids, otherwise it will be too firm and taste too bitter as no sugar is added.

CRÈME CARAMEL

Here is a classic dish that is so easy to make. I have made these in ramekins as they are easier to turn out than a whole dish. Not suitable for freezing.

- Serves 6

> 110 g (4 oz) granulated sugar
> 4 eggs
> 50 g (2 oz) caster sugar
> 600 ml (1 pint) full fat milk
> ½ tsp vanilla extract

You will need six size 1 (150 ml/¼ pint) ramekins, well greased and sitting in a roasting tin on a piece of kitchen paper to stop the ramekins sliding around.

Measure the granulated sugar with 150 ml (¼ pint) of water into a stainless steel saucepan.

TWO-, THREE- AND FOUR-OVEN AGA Heat the saucepan on the simmering plate, stirring until all the sugar has dissolved. Once dissolved, transfer to the boiling plate and boil without stirring until the water has evaporated (you will know this as the pan goes quiet!) and the sugar turns to a golden caramel – this should take about 4 minutes.

CONVENTIONAL OVEN Heat the saucepan at a low temperature on the hob, stirring until all the sugar has dissolved. Once dissolved, turn up the heat on the hob and boil without stirring, until the water has evaporated (follow as above).

Pour the caramel into the ramekins and leave to set hard while making the custard.

Break the eggs into a mixing bowl and whisk by hand with the caster sugar until well combined. Measure the milk and vanilla into a pan and heat gently on the simmering plate (or hob), until hand hot. Pour on to the eggs and whisk by hand until combined. Butter the ramekins above the caramel layer, sieve the custard and pour into the ramekins. Pour boiling water into the roasting tin until it comes half way up the ramekins – this is called a bain marie.

TWO-, THREE- AND FOUR-OVEN AGA Slide the bain marie roasting tin on to the lowest set of runners in the roasting oven. Bake for 8–10 minutes, until starting to set but still soft in the middle. Transfer to the simmering oven for a further 20–30 minutes, until just set on top but with a slight wobble in the middle (will firm up when cold).

CONVENTIONAL OVEN Bake the bain marie in a preheated oven (160°C/140°C Fan/Gas 3) for 25–30 minutes, until just set on top but with a slight wobble in the middle.

Transfer to the fridge and leave overnight (they can be made 2 days in advance). To serve, run a knife around the edge, invert a plate on the ramekin and turn out on to the plate.

Secret

- The moisture from the set custard will soften the caramel, so you need to chill it overnight as a minimum to allow the caramel to become runny.

CRÈME BRULÉE

This recipe is for my lovely friend Debs – her favourite dessert! It is often said that you cannot make crème brulée in an Aga as it doesn't have a grill. Well the grill bit is true, but you can still make it just by making a caramel in a pan and pouring it over the top of the set cold custard. Not suitable for freezing.

- Serves 6

4 egg yolks	600 ml (1 pint) single cream
25 g (1 oz) caster sugar	110 g (4 oz) granulated sugar
1 tsp vanilla extract	

You will need six size 1 (150 ml/¼ pint) ramekins, sitting in a roasting tin on a piece of kitchen paper to stop the ramekins sliding around.

Measure the egg yolks, caster sugar and vanilla in a bowl and whisk lightly with a hand whisk until combined. Heat the cream in a pan on the simmering plate (or hob), until just under simmering point (hand hot), gradually pour on to the egg yolks and whisk to combine. Sieve the custard into a jug and pour into the prepared ramekins.

Pour boiling water from the kettle into the roasting tin until it comes half way up the sides of the ramekins – this is called a bain marie.

TWO-, THREE- AND FOUR-OVEN AGA Slide the bain marie roasting tin on to the lowest set of runners in the roasting oven. Cook for 8–10 minutes and then transfer to the simmering oven for 45 minutes, until set around the edge but with a slight wobble in the middle.

To make the brulée, heat the saucepan on the simmering plate, stirring until all the sugar has dissolved. Once dissolved, transfer to the boiling plate and boil without stirring until the water has evaporated (you will know this as the pan goes quiet!) and the sugar turns to a golden caramel – this could take about 4 minutes. Pour immediately on to the set cold custard and tip the ramekins so the caramel reaches the sides.

CONVENTIONAL OVEN Bake the bain marie in a preheated oven (160°C/140°C Fan/Gas 3) for about 30 minutes. Sprinkle the set custard with a tablespoon of demerara sugar on each and slide under a preheated grill to bubble.

Remove the ramekins from the baking tin and set aside to cool. Transfer to the fridge for up to 5 hours (to allow the caramel to soften) or keep at room temperature for up to 7 hours. Serve at room temperature or gently warmed in the simmering oven for 10 minutes.

Secret

- Caramel cannot be made in a non-stick pan because it will not change colour, so use stainless steel, aluminium or copper.
- The Aga method of making caramel is a smooth topping, so if you like it grainy, sprinkle a little demerara sugar on the set custard and then pour the caramel on top. When the caramel sets, it is like glass, so needs about 5 hours to soften a little. But do not leave overnight in the fridge otherwise the caramel will turn to liquid.

FRESH STRAWBERRY SOUFFLÉ

So many people are scared of making soufflés, but this recipe really is quick to make and to bake and tastes delicious too. Not suitable for freezing.

- Serves 6

>   300 g (10 oz) strawberries, hulled and halved
>   110 g (4 oz) caster sugar, plus 1 tbsp
>   1 heaped tbsp cornflour
>   3 tbsp crème de fraise or blackcurrant crème de cassis liqueur
>   3 egg whites
>   Icing sugar, for dusting

You will need six size 1 (150 ml/¼ pint) ramekins, buttered.

Measure the strawberries into a saucepan with two tablespoons of water and 110 g (4 oz) of the caster sugar and gently heat on the simmering plate (or hob). Cover with a lid and transfer to the simmering oven (or reduce the heat on the hob) and leave for 10 minutes, until just tender. Mash with a potato masher just enough to combine the fruit and syrup.

Combine the cornflour and crème de fraise (or cassis) in a small bowl or cup and mix with a teaspoon until smooth and pour on to the strawberries in the pan and stir briskly. Return the pan to the heat and simmer for 1–2 minutes, continuously whisking until it bubbles for a minute. Set aside to cool a little.

Measure the egg whites into a large bowl (or the bowl of a free-standing machine). Whisk on high speed with a hand-held electric mixer (or in the free-standing machine), until white and fluffy, like cloud. Still whisking on maximum speed, gradually add the sugar, a teaspoon at a time, until it is well incorporated and the meringue is stiff and shiny and stands upright on the whisk.

Fold the strawberry purée into the egg whites and fold until smooth, taking care not to knock any air out of the egg whites. Spoon into the ramekins and level the top.

TWO-, THREE- AND FOUR-OVEN AGA Preheat a baking sheet in the roasting oven until it is very hot. Sit the ramekins on top of the baking sheet and slide on to the grid shelf on the floor of the roasting oven. Bake for 8–10 minutes, until well risen.

CONVENTIONAL OVEN Bake on a hot baking sheet in a preheated oven (190°C/170°C Fan/ Gas 5) for 8–10 minutes, until well risen.

Dust with icing sugar and serve at once.

Secret

- Run your finger around the sides of the ramekin near the top just before baking, this helps the soufflé to rise evenly.

CORNISH BEAUTIES

This is for my lovely friends Ali and Tanya, who both live in Cornwall. It is a great recipe that contains apples and oat biscuits, making it truly Cornish. Not suitable for freezing.

- Serves 6

    4 dessert apples, peeled, cored and cut into small cubes
    2 tsp ground cinnamon
    50 g (2 oz) caster sugar
    150 ml (¼ pint) double cream, lightly whipped
    4 tbsp brandy
    2 tbsp lemon juice
    8 oat biscuits, crushed (see secret, below)

You will need six stemmed glasses.

Measure the apple, cinnamon and sugar into a small saucepan. Heat on the simmering plate (or hob) for a few minutes, cover and transfer to the simmering oven (or turn down the heat on the hob) for about 30 minutes, until the apples are soft. Mash using a potato masher until smooth and set aside to cool.

Spoon one tablespoon of the apple purée into the base of six wine glasses. Add the remaining apple purée into the whipped cream and stir in the brandy and lemon juice.

Divide half of the crushed biscuits into the glasses on top of the apple purée. Then divide the apple cream mixture between the glasses and finish with a layer of the remaining crushed biscuits. Chill for 1 hour and serve chilled.

Can be kept in the fridge for up to 6 hours.

Secret

- The easiest way to crush biscuits for this recipe or for a crumb crust is to put them in a plastic bag and bash with a rolling pin or the base of a saucepan.

MARMALADE AND FRUIT SPONGE PUDDINGS

These are full of dried fruit with a glaze of marmalade. Made individually they are quick to cook and perfect for serving lots of people as the recipe is easy to double up. Not suitable for freezing.

- Serves 6

> 2 eggs
> 110 g (4 oz) self-raising flour
> 110 g (4 oz) caster sugar
> 110 g (4 oz) butter, softened
> ½ tsp baking powder
> 50 g (2 oz) sultanas
> 50 g (2 oz) ready-to-eat dried apricots, snipped into raisin-sized pieces
> 50 g (2 oz) ready-to-eat prunes, snipped into raisin-sized pieces
> Finely grated zest and juice of 1 large orange
> 6 tbsp finely cut orange marmalade

You will need six size 1 (150 ml/¼ pint) ramekins or timbale moulds, greased well.

To make the sponge, measure the eggs, flour, sugar, butter, baking powder, dried fruit and orange zest into a mixing bowl and beat well with a wooden spoon or a hand-held electric mixer, until smooth.

Mix the marmalade with two tablespoons of the orange juice (reserve the rest) and spoon equally into the base of each ramekin. Spoon the sponge mixture on top and level the surface. Arrange the ramekins on a baking sheet.

TWO-OVEN AGA Slide on to the grid shelf on the floor of the roasting oven with the cold sheet on the second set of runners. Bake for 20 minutes, until golden and risen.

THREE- AND FOUR-OVEN AGA Slide on to the grid shelf on the floor of the baking oven. Bake for 25 minutes. If getting too brown, slide the cold sheet on to the second set of runners.

CONVENTIONAL OVEN Bake in a preheated oven (180°C/160°C Fan/Gas 4) for 20 minutes.

Leave to cool slightly, then run a palette knife around the edge of the ramekins and invert on to a plate. Pour the reserved orange juice over the hot sponges and serve immediately with custard or cream.

Secret

- You can replace the fruits with others of your choice, such as cherries, raisins and dates, but make sure the total weight adds up to the same as above.

ZINGY LEMON DESSERT

This is so lemony and is refreshing and creamy too. The pudding looks particularly smart as it is made in cooking rings, which can be bought from all good kitchen shops and looks very professional too. Not suitable for freezing.

- Serves 6

> 450 ml (¾ pint) double cream
> 75 g (3 oz) caster sugar
> Finely grated zest and juice of 2 lemons
> 4 trifle sponges
> Mint leaves, to decorate (optional)

You will need six 7 cm (2¾ in) cooking rings. Arrange on a tray or small baking sheet lined with cling film.

Measure the cream, sugar and lemon zest into a shallow saucepan. Bring to the boil, stirring, on the boiling plate (or hob). Set aside for about 5 minutes and then add the lemon juice, stirring until combined and the mixture naturally thickens slightly.

Slice the sponges horizontally and cut in half lengthways. Trim the pieces so they fit neatly into the cooking rings in a single layer. Spoon over the lemon mixture and level the top. Transfer to the fridge for a minimum of 4 hours to set.

To serve, sit each dessert on a plate and carefully remove the rings. Decorate each with grated lemon zest or a sprig of mint or serve with Lemon Twists or Mini Florentines (see pages 144 and 140).

Secret

- These can be made up to 24 hours ahead and kept covered in cling film in the fridge.

PANNACOTTA WITH LEMON AND PASSION FRUIT

Pannacotta means 'cooked cream' and should be just set and smooth. I have made these ones in ramekins, which you turn out, but if you prefer, serve the pudding in individual glasses. I ate a similar pannacotta to this one in a lovely restaurant in France – they served the set pannacotta in curvy glasses with a passion fruit coulis layer on top – delicious! Not suitable for freezing.

- Serves 6

>   2 tsp powdered gelatine
>   600 ml (1 pint) single cream
>   50 g (2 oz) caster sugar
>   1 tsp vanilla extract
>   4 passion fruit, halved, to serve
>   2 tbsp good quality lemon curd (or see Luxury Lemon Curd on page 153)
>   Mint sprigs, to decorate

You will need six size 1 (150 ml/¼ pint) ramekins. Lightly oil them and invert on to kitchen paper for any excess oil to drain away.

Measure three tablespoons of water into a small bowl and sprinkle over the gelatine. Let the gelatine soak up all the liquid for a few minutes and turn to sponge. Once sponged, sit the bowl on the back of the Aga (or in a bowl of boiling water) and leave until the gelatine has dissolved and become liquid.

Measure the cream and sugar into a saucepan and bring the cream to just below boiling on the simmering plate (or hob), stirring to dissolve the sugar. Remove from the heat, cool very slightly, add the vanilla extract and stir in the dissolved gelatine.

Sieve the cream into the ramekins, cover with cling film and leave to set in the fridge for a minimum of 6 hours or overnight.

Scoop the seeds and juice from the passion fruit into a sieve and press with a teaspoon so all the juice falls into a jug. Discard the seeds and mix with the juice with the lemon curd.

To serve the pannacotta, use your index finger to release them from the side of each ramekin and turn upside down on to a plate. Serve a spoonful of the passion fruit mixture on top. Decorate with mint and serve chilled.

Secret

- Usually when making a mousse in a ramekin or mould that needs to be turned out, I line the mould with cling film. However, a pannacotta is a smooth creamy texture and the cling film would leave an unattractive pattern on the top, hence just oiling the mould instead.

GIN AND TONIC JELLY

OK girls, this one is for you! This is perfect for a girlie night and as well as being seriously potent, it is luminous to boot. Can be made and kept in ramekins up to 3 days ahead and kept in the fridge. Not suitable for freezing.

- Serves 6–8

  1 x 135 g packet lemon jelly
  100 ml (3½ fl oz) gin
  200 ml (7 fl oz) tonic water

You will need six size 1 (150 ml/¼ pint) ramekins or timbale moulds or serve in eight smaller glasses and don't turn out.

Break the jelly cubes into a measuring jug and pour enough boiling water from the kettle to make up to 300 ml (½ pint). Stir and sit on the back of the Aga (or stir briskly) to dissolve the jelly cubes.

Add the gin and tonic to the jelly in the jug and stir. Then pour the jelly into the ramekins and transfer to the fridge to set for a minimum of 6 hours.

Carefully loosen the jelly around the edge and invert on to a plate. Serve with cream or a scoop of zingy Lemon and Lime Sorbet (see page 115).

Secrets

- When releasing the jelly to turn out, use your finger to pull the jelly away from the sides of the ramekins so the air reaches the base, the jellies should then easily come out.

- As this is a fun dessert, use unusual shaped moulds instead of ramekins.

Naughties

These beautiful sweet treats are lovely at the end of a meal with a cup of coffee, or can provide a naughty and indulgent gift for any friend — wrapped with tissue and ribbon, they are irresistible.

MINI FLORENTINES

These crisp nutty biscuits with a chocolate coating are the ultimate naughty treat to be served with dessert or coffee and are very impressive to serve to your guests. They can be made and kept in the fridge up to 4 days ahead. Freeze well.

- Makes 20
  - 25 g (1 oz) butter
  - 25 g (1 oz) demerara sugar
  - 25 g (1 oz) golden syrup
  - 25 g (1 oz) plain flour
  - 2 glacé cherries, finely chopped
  - 25 g (1 oz) hazelnuts, finely chopped
  - 25 g (1 oz) almonds, finely chopped
  - 75 g (3 oz) plain chocolate

You will need a baking sheet, lined with non-stick baking parchment.

Measure the butter, sugar and syrup into a small pan and heat gently on the simmering plate (or hob), until the butter has melted. Remove from the heat, add the flour, chopped cherries and nuts. Stir well with a wooden spoon until all the nuts are coated.

Make 20 little balls (or 20 teaspoonfuls) and arrange on the prepared baking sheet, not too close together as they spread a little.

Two-oven Aga Slide on to the grid shelf on the floor of the roasting oven with the cold sheet on the second set of runners. Bake for 10–12 minutes, until golden brown and flat.

Three- and four-oven Aga Slide on to the grid shelf on the floor of the baking oven. Bake for 12–15 minutes, until flattened and golden brown.

Conventional oven Bake in a preheated oven (180°C/160°C Fan/Gas 4) for 10 minutes, until golden brown and flat.

Allow to cool for a few minutes, then transfer to a cooling rack using a fish slice. Melt the chocolate in a heatproof bowl on the back of the Aga (or over a pan of simmering water on the hob).

Using a baby palette knife or the back of a teaspoon, spread the flat side of each florentine with chocolate. For a professional finish, mark a zigzag in the chocolate using a fork. Lay on the cooling rack, chocolate side up to set.

Secret

- For a variation, make some with white chocolate and some with plain chocolate.

CINNAMON SHORTBREAD

I use semolina in my shortbread to give a lovely crunch, but if you haven't got any, you can use cornflour instead. Freeze well.

- Makes 12 shortbread wedges
    175 g (6 oz) plain flour
    175 g (6 oz) butter, softened
    75 g (3 oz) caster sugar
    75 g (3 oz) semolina
    1½ tsp ground cinnamon
    1 tbsp demerara sugar

You will need a 20 cm (8 in) sandwich cake tin, greased.

Measure the flour, butter, caster sugar, semolina and cinnamon into a processor and process until the mixture is thoroughly combined and comes together to form a dough. This can also be done by hand, rubbing the butter into the flour first then adding the sugar, semolina and cinnamon and working the ingredients together to form a ball of mixture.

Press the mixture into the prepared tin and level with the back of a spoon. Score the top of the shortbread into 12 evenly spaced wedges. Prick each wedge evenly with a fork and then sprinkle the top with the demerara sugar.

Two-, THREE- AND FOUR-OVEN AGA Slide on to the grid shelf on the floor of the roasting oven with the cold sheet on the second set of runners. Bake for about 10 minutes, until a pale golden colour. Transfer to the simmering oven for about 35-45 minutes, until firm to the touch.

CONVENTIONAL OVEN Bake in a preheated oven (160°C/140°C Fan/Gas 3) for 30–40 minutes, until the shortbread is a pale golden colour and cooked through.

Allow the shortbread to cool in the tin for a few minutes then cut through the score marks into 12 even wedges. Once completely cold, carefully lift out of the tin and transfer on to a wire rack. Store in an airtight tin.

Secret

- You must cut the shortbread into wedges while still warm otherwise it will crumble.

LEMON AND MINT BISCUITS

These are similar in texture to shortbread and fresh and zesty. They are perfect served with any mousse or fruit salad. Freeze well.

- Makes 40 biscuits
    175 g (6 oz) butter, softened
    Finely grated zest of 1 lemon and 2 tbsp lemon juice
    2 tbsp chopped fresh mint
    110 g (4 oz) caster sugar
    225 g (8 oz) plain flour
    25 g (1 oz) demerara sugar

You will need three baking sheets, lightly greased.

Measure the butter, lemon zest and juice, mint and caster sugar into a mixing bowl and beat with a wooden spoon until light and fluffy. Stir in the flour, bringing the mixture together with your hands and kneading lightly until smooth.

Divide the mixture into two and roll out to form two 15 cm (6 in) sausage shapes. Roll the biscuit 'sausages' in the demerara sugar to evenly coat and then wrap in non-stick baking parchment or foil and chill in the fridge until firm.

Cut each 'sausage' into about 20 slices, each 5 mm ($^1/_4$ in) thick, and put on to the prepared baking sheets, allowing a little room for them to spread.

TWO-OVEN AGA Slide on to the grid shelf on the floor of the roasting oven with the cold sheet on the second set of runners. Bake for 10–12 minutes, until pale golden brown.

THREE- AND FOUR-OVEN AGA Slide on to the grid shelf on the floor of the baking oven. Bake for 12–15 minutes. If the biscuits are browning too quickly, slide the cold sheet on to the second set of runners.

CONVENTIONAL OVEN Bake in a preheated oven (160°C/140°C Fan/Gas 3) for 10–12 minutes.

Lift the biscuits on to a cooling rack with a fish slice and leave to cool completely.

Secret

- Wrap the rolled biscuit in foil or baking paper and not cling film otherwise the roll will sweat and be oily.

LEMON TWISTS

These sweet versions of cheese straws — but with a twist — are particularly quick to make because ready rolled puff pastry is used. Freeze well.

- Makes 20 twists
  - I x 375 g packet ready rolled puff pastry
  - 2 good tbsp good quality lemon curd (or see Luxury Lemon Curd on
    - page 153)
  - 2 tbsp caster sugar
  - Finely grated zest of I lemon
  - I egg, beaten
  - 2 good tbsp demerara sugar

You will need a baking sheet, lined with non-stick baking parchment.

Lay the pastry out on a floured worksurface and re-roll to a slightly larger rectangle so it is about 3 mm ($^1/_8$ in) thick, and about 25 x 40 cm (10 x 16 in) in size. Cut the pastry in half lengthways to make two rectangular pieces.

Spread the lemon curd on one side of one of the rectangles. Sprinkle the caster sugar and lemon zest on top of the lemon curd. Sit the other pastry piece on top and re-roll slightly, just enough to squidge the pastry pieces together. Chill for at least 10 minutes.

Trim the edges, brush with the beaten egg and sprinkle with the demerara sugar. Cut widthways into about 20 straws, each 2 cm ($^3/_4$ in) wide. Give each straw a double twist and arrange on the prepared baking sheet.

TWO-, THREE- AND FOUR-OVEN AGA Slide on to the grid shelf on the floor of the roasting oven. Bake for about 12 minutes, until golden brown and crisp. Remove the grid shelf and transfer directly to the floor of the oven for about 3 minutes to crispen underneath.

CONVENTIONAL OVEN Bake in a preheated oven (200°C/180°C Fan/Gas 6) for 12–15 minutes, until golden.

Transfer to a cooling rack to cool completely and serve with mousses or coffee.

Secret

- To help the twists stay in their shape, press down the ends slightly when arranging on the baking sheet before baking. You can also cook them un-twisted just in strips, but the twists look very impressive!

BISCOTTI

These Italian biscuits are traditionally hard and crunchy, the name meaning twice-cooked ('bis' is Italian for twice and 'cotti' for cooked), making them ideal for dipping in dessert wine, coffee or a shot of brandy, whisky or rum.

- Makes 30 biscuits

  225 g (8 oz) plain flour

  A pinch of salt

  1 tsp bicarbonate of soda

  1 tsp cream of tartar

  225 g (8 oz) demerara sugar

  3 eggs

  50 g (2 oz) whole pistachio nuts

  75 g (3 oz) chopped almonds

  75 g (3 oz) sultanas

  1 tsp almond extract

  Icing sugar, for dusting

You will need a baking sheet, lined with non-stick baking parchment.

Measure all the ingredients, except the icing sugar, into a large bowl and mix with a wooden spoon until combined.

Tip on to a floured worksurface and knead lightly to make a fairly sticky soft dough. Divide the mixture into three and roll each third into a sausage shape, about 18 x 5 cm (7 x 2 in). Arrange on the baking sheet, leaving a space between each sausage.

TWO-, THREE- AND FOUR-OVEN AGA   Slide on to the grid shelf on the floor of the roasting oven. Bake for 20–25 minutes, until light golden brown and firm. Remove from the Aga on to a breadboard and slice each sausage into 2 cm (¾ in) slices on the diagonal, making 30 slices in all. Return to the baking sheet and slide into the simmering oven for about 30 minutes, until firm and crisp (not soft in the middle).

CONVENTIONAL OVEN   Bake in a preheated oven (180°C/160°C Fan/Gas 4) for about 25 minutes, until golden. Remove from the oven on to a breadboard and slice each sausage into 2 cm (¾ in) slices on the diagonal, making 30 slices in all. Return to the baking sheet, turn down the oven temperature to 140°C/120°C Fan/Gas 1 and bake for 10–15 minutes, until firm and crisp (not soft in the middle).

Transfer to a wire rack to cool. Dust with icing sugar to serve.

Secrets

- The traditional biscotti recipe is made with hazelnuts and aniseed, but they are now flavoured with a wide variety of nuts and other flavourings. You can vary my choice of nuts if you wish.

- These biscuits are delicious dipped into Frangelico, a sweet hazelnut liqueur, or Kahlúa served in a shot glass.

TRUE VANILLA FUDGE

This vanilla fudge is perfect for cutting into squares and serving after a meal; or pack into a Kilner jar, tie with a pretty ribbon and give as a present. Can be kept in the fridge for up to 3 weeks. Not suitable for freezing.

- Makes 24 squares

    300 ml (¹/₂ pint) full fat milk
    350 g (12 oz) caster sugar
    110 g (4 oz) butter, cubed
    1 vanilla pod, split lengthways

You will need a 900 g (2 lb) loaf tin, lined with cling film.

Measure the milk, sugar and butter into a saucepan. Using a teaspoon, scrape the seeds from the split vanilla pod and add to the saucepan.

Bring to the boil on the simmering plate (or hob), continuously stirring until the sugar and butter have dissolved. Allow to reduce and boil (without a lid) for about 15 minutes, until it has thickened and turned a pale caramel colour.

To test if the fudge is ready for setting, spoon a little mixture into a glass of cold water and if it forms a ball, it is ready; if not, continue to boil for a little longer.

Set the pan aside to cool for a few minutes. Then stir with a wooden spoon and spoon into the prepared loaf tin. Transfer to the fridge for a minimum of 4 hours to set firm.

Tip upside down on to a wooden board, remove the cling film and cut into 24 squares or whichever size or shape you like.

Secrets

- With Aga cooking I always try to cook in the ovens rather than on top to keep the heat in the Aga. However, I have tried making this fudge in the simmering oven, but it does not reduce or thicken so it is easiest to simmer it on the plate.

- If you have a sugar thermometer, sit it in the pan once the sugar has dissolved. The boiling liquid should reach 113-118°C, which is 'soft ball' stage.

SCOTTISH TABLET

This is a traditional Scottish sweet – similar to fudge, but slightly firmer and sweeter. You have to be on the ball with this recipe, keeping an eye on it and once ready, whisk immediately and turn into the tin otherwise it will set in the pan. My friend Bid is an expert at making this recipe, so I did ring her for advice while making it! Keeps for up to a month in the fridge in a sealed container.

- Makes 30 pieces

450 g (1 lb) granulated sugar	150 ml (¼ pint) milk
50 g (2 oz) butter	170 g can of full fat condensed milk

You will need a small Aga roasting tin or traybake tin measuring 30 x 23 cm (12 x 9 in). Cut a rectangle of non-stick baking parchment just larger than the base and sides of the tin and cut each corner with scissors to the depth of the tin. Grease the tin with butter and then line with the baking parchment, pushing it neatly into the corners to fit.

Plug a hand-held electric mixer into the mains and sit a trivet or board next to it.

Measure all the ingredients into a large, deep saucepan. Melt on the simmering plate (or on the hob at a moderate heat), stirring until the sugar has dissolved. Leave to boil for about 15 minutes, during which time it will naturally darken in colour. Do not worry if you see flecks of darker caramel, these will disappear when whisked.

To test if the tablet is ready for setting, spoon a little mixture into a glass of cold water and if it forms a ball, it is ready; if not, continue to boil for a little longer. (If you like to use a sugar thermometer, see the secret on page 148.)

Sit the pan on the trivet or board, and immediately whisk with a hand-held mixer, until the mixture thickens and starts to stick to the sides of the pan. Be careful not to overbeat otherwise the sweet becomes dry.

Spoon into the roasting (or traybake) tin and level the top. Leave to set for about 5 minutes, then cut into squares (it's very sweet, so I cut it into small squares). Transfer to the fridge to become rock hard and then break off the squares.

Secret

- The saucepan needs to be very deep so the boiling liquid does not spit or boil over.

Variations

Cherry tablet: Add one tablespoon of finely chopped glacé cherries just before putting in the tin.

Ginger tablet: Add one tablespoon of finely chopped stem ginger just before putting in the tin.

Vanilla tablet: Add a few drops of vanilla extract just before whisking.

Walnut tablet: Add one tablespoon of finely chopped walnuts just before putting in the tin.

RICH PISTACHIO TRUFFLES

Good to serve as a special treat with coffee or after a meal, it is very important to use 70% cocoa solids plain chocolate for these truffles, otherwise they will not set easily. The rolled completed truffles will keep in the fridge for up to 10 days. The plain truffles, not coated, freeze well.

- Makes 24 truffles
    - 150 g (5 oz) plain chocolate, 70% cocoa solids
    - 150 ml (¼ pint) double cream
    - 1–2 tbsp brandy
    - 2 tbsp icing sugar
    - 50 g (2 oz) pistachio nuts, finely chopped

You will need a shallow plastic container about 10 x 15 cm (4 x 6 in) and petit four cases for the truffles.

Measure the chocolate, cream and brandy into a heatproof bowl and sit on the back of the Aga (or over a saucepan of just simmering water) to melt. Do not allow the mixture to get too hot, stir occasionally with a teaspoon. Once melted, stir in the icing sugar, which will dissolve in the warm mixture.

Pour into the plastic container and set aside to cool. Then place in the fridge for a minimum of 2 hours to become firm.

Cut the set chocolate mixture into 24 even squares and roll into a ball using your hands. Then roll in the chopped pistachios and sit each truffle in a petit four case.

Secret

- You must melt the brandy (or any alcohol) with the chocolate from the beginning so they are always the same temperature. If you add alcohol to melted hot chocolate, the mixture will become thick and lumpy.

Variations

Colour: Instead of using nuts, roll the truffles in cocoa powder or icing sugar to give a nice pretty contrast.

Dried fruit: You can either replace the nuts with chopped dried fruit or sprinkle dried fruit on the top. Dried apricots, dates and cranberries work well, but should be chopped finely.

Fresh fruit: When rolling the truffle pop a blueberry or small raspberry in the centre and re-roll so the fruit is completely encased in the fruit. These will only keep in the fridge for about 48 hours.

More chocolate: For very rich sumptuous truffles, dip half a truffle in melted white chocolate to give a great effect and a crunchy outside. Leave on baking parchment to set in the fridge.

Nuts: You can replace the pistachios with any finely chopped nuts – hazelnuts, almonds and macadamia nuts work well.

Turkish truffles: Use the same method as for the fruit truffles, but cut a small square of Turkish delight sweet and push into the centre of the truffle.

PEPPERMINT CREAMS

Such a treat with coffee and so simple to make. They freeze well too.

- Makes 36 peppermint creams

      I egg white
      $^1/_2$ tsp peppermint extract
      350 g (12 oz) icing sugar, sieved

Whisk the egg white with a hand-held electric mixer, until frothy like a cloud. Add the peppermint extract and half of the sieved icing sugar. Whisk again until smooth, add the remaining icing sugar and then whisk again until the mixture just comes together.

Tip on to a worksurface, dust lightly with icing sugar and knead to a soft dough (like pastry). Using a rolling pin, roll out to a 15 x 15 cm (6 x 6 in) square and then slice into 36 small squares and sit them on a wire rack to dry out for 1–2 hours, turning over halfway through.

Keep in the fridge until they are ready to be devoured (up to 4 days).

Secrets

- Buy peppermint extract and not essence otherwise they will taste artificial and not fresh.

- To make them extra fancy, once dried out, dip the creams in melted plain chocolate and leave to set.

Sauces

LUXURY LEMON CURD

- Makes 3 x 450 g (1 lb) jars
    3 eggs
    Finely grated zest and juice of
        3 lemons
    110 g (4 oz) butter, softened
    225 g (8 oz) caster sugar

Measure all the ingredients into a mixing bowl and whisk together by hand until combined (don't worry if the butter is not completely smooth).

TWO-, THREE- AND FOUR-OVEN AGA
Cover with cling film and transfer to the simmering oven for about 1 hour. Remove the cling film (the contents will still be runny) and whisk again to combine. Return to the simmering oven for a further hour until thickened.

CONVENTIONAL OVEN Make in a heatproof bowl over a saucepan of gently simmering water, whisking for about 5 minutes, until combined. Stir and spoon into sterilised jars. Label and keep in the fridge for up to 4 weeks.

BUTTERSCOTCH SAUCE

- Makes about 300 ml (½ pint)
    175 g (6 oz) caster sugar
    110 g (4 oz) butter
    150 ml (¼ pint) double cream
    2 tsp vanilla extract

Measure the sugar and butter into a pan, heat on the simmering plate (or hob), until the sugar has dissolved and butter melted. Add the cream and bring to the boil on the boiling plate (or turn up the heat on the hob), stirring, and boil for a couple of minutes. Stir in the vanilla extract. Keeps well in the fridge for up to 3 days. Thickens in the fridge, so if making ahead, sit on the back of the Aga to become pouring consistency (or gently heat in a pan on the hob).

LUXURY BRANDY SAUCE

- Makes about 900 ml (1½ pints)
    50 g (2 oz) butter
    25 g (1 oz) plain flour
    600 ml (1 pint) milk
    150 ml (¼ pint) double cream
    50 g (2 oz) caster sugar
    4–5 tbsp brandy

Melt the butter in a pan on the simmering plate (or hob). Off the heat, whisk in the flour to make a roux. Return to the heat, gradually whisk in the milk and cream until boiling, whisking continuously. Add the sugar and brandy and bring to the boil once more. Serve hot. This is a coating sauce, if you like yours a little thicker, add 15 g (½ oz) more plain flour to the roux. Keeps for up to 24 hours in the fridge.

MALIBU SAUCE

- Makes 450 ml (³/₄ pint)
  - 110 g (4 oz) light muscovado sugar
  - 6 tbsp Malibu rum
  - 300 ml (½ pint) double cream

Measure all the ingredients into a pan. Bring to the boil on the boiling plate (or hob), transfer to the simmering plate (or turn down the heat on the hob) and simmer for a few minutes, stirring continuously. Ideally serve warm, cover with cling film and leave in the simmering oven (or keep in the pan and reheat when serving) for about 30 minutes to keep warm. Keeps well in the fridge for up to 2 days. Reheat gently in a pan to serve.

TOFFEE AND SULTANA SAUCE

- Makes 300 ml (½ pint)
  - 110 g (4 oz) light muscovado sugar
  - 50g (2 oz) butter
  - 150 ml (¼ pint) double cream
  - 50 g (2 oz) sultanas

Measure the sugar, butter and cream into a pan and stir on the boiling plate (or hob), until completely melted and combined. Stir in the sultanas and serve hot or cold. Keeps in the fridge for up to 2 days. Reheat gently in a pan to serve.

REAL CUSTARD

- Makes 600 ml (1 pint)
  - 5 egg yolks
  - 25 g (1 oz) caster sugar
  - 2 tsp cornflour
  - 450 ml (¾ pint) milk
  - 150 ml (¼ pint) double cream
  - 1 vanilla pod, seeds scraped from the centre

Measure the egg yolks, sugar and cornflour into a bowl and whisk with a hand whisk until smooth. Measure the milk, cream and vanilla seeds into a small pan and bring to the boil on the simmering plate (or hob), stirring continuously. Pour the hot milk on to the egg yolk mixture and whisk until smooth. Sieve back into the pan and heat on the simmering plate (or hob), stirring until it coats the back of the spoon. Be careful not to boil rapidly otherwise the egg yolks will curdle. Pour into a jug, cover in cling film and keep in the simmering oven to serve warm. Keeps in the fridge for 2 days. Reheat gently in a pan to serve.

BRANDY CREAM

- Makes 300 ml (½ pint)
  - 300 ml (½ pint) double cream, whipped
  - 50 g (2 oz) icing sugar
  - 3 tbsp brandy

Measure all the ingredients together into a bowl and stir until combined. Keep in the fridge for up to 2 days.

BRANDY BUTTER

- Makes about 225 g (8 oz)
  - 75 g (3 oz) chilled butter, cubed
  - 175 g (6 oz) icing sugar
  - 3 tbsp brandy

Measure the butter and icing sugar into a processor and whiz until combined. Still whizzing, add the brandy through the lid tube until creamy and smooth. If you add too much brandy and it curdles, add a little more butter and icing sugar until smooth. To make by hand, use softened butter and beat in a mixing bowl with the sugar and two and a half tablespoons of brandy. Using chilled butter in the processor means you can add more brandy! Keeps for up to a month in the fridge.

APRICOT COULIS

- Makes about 600 ml (1 pint)
  150 g (5 oz) ready-to-eat
    dried apricots
  2 tbsp orange juice
  450 ml ¾ pint) boiling water
    in a jug

Measure the apricots, orange juice and 100 ml (3½ fl oz) of the boiling water into a bowl, cover with cling film and transfer to the simmering oven (or a warm place) for about 30 minutes to plump up. Transfer the apricots and any liquid in the bowl into a processor and whiz until smooth. Pour the remaining water (which, by now, will be tepid) gently through the funnel while the mixer is whizzing to give a smooth coulis. Sieve and serve cold. Keeps in the fridge for up to 4 days.

SOFT SUMMER FRUIT COULIS

- Makes 300 ml (½ pint)
  450 g (1 lb) soft fruits, such
    as raspberries, blackberries,
    strawberries or redcurrants
  2 tbsp icing sugar
  Juice of ½ lemon

Measure the fruits, sugar and lemon juice into a processor and whiz until smooth. Sieve and serve cold. Keeps in the fridge for up to 2 days.

WHITE CHOCOLATE SAUCE

- Makes 450 ml (¾ pint)
  150 g (5 oz) 100% Belgian white
    chocolate
  300 ml (½ pint) double cream

Measure the chocolate and cream into a jug or bowl and sit on the back of the Aga (or set the bowl over a pan of gently simmering water), stirring occasionally until melted. Stir until smooth and do not allow to get too hot. Serve at room temperature so it is a pouring consistency. Keeps well in the fridge for up to 2 days. It will thicken up in the fridge so sit on the back of the Aga to loosen up to serve, or reheat gently in a pan to serve.

OLD-FASHIONED CHOCOLATE SAUCE

- Makes 300 ml (½ pint)
  110 g (4 oz) caster sugar
  50 g (2 oz) cocoa powder

Measure the sugar into a pan, add 250 ml (9 fl oz) water and heat on the simmering plate (or hob) to dissolve the sugar. Once dissolved, bring to the boil, add the cocoa and continue to heat, stirring until smooth. Set aside and it will thicken slightly when cool. Keeps well in the fridge for up to 4 days.

Lucy Young is the new young Aga talent. She has a *Cordon Bleu* training and has worked with Mary Berry for over 19 years, helping create and test Mary's recipes for books and TV and teaching at her very popular Aga workshops. Lucy has often appeared on the UKTV Food Channel and is regularly interviewed on radio. She is the author of *Secrets from a Country Kitchen, Secrets of Aga Cakes* and *Tips for Better Baking* also published by Ebury.

BIG THANK YOU

Firstly to Lucinda Kaizik who assists me with my demonstrations and has helped me every step of the way with this book – helping to test recipes and remember all that I forget! Thanks Missy, you know I couldn't do it without you, we are a team and you are a special friend too.

Carey Smith and Vicky Orchard at Ebury Press – Carey has commissioned all my Ebury books and I am forever grateful to her for her faith and support in me in this competitive market. Emma Callery, who edited this book with perfect perfection and patience. Will Heap for the stunning photos and Anna Burges-Lumsden, the home economist for the photo shoot, who has beautifully translated my recipes into photos. Michele Topham, at my agents Felicity Bryan, who gives me never-ending advice and support. Dawn Roads from Aga who is Aga through and through.

To my friends and wonderful family who again have walked by my side and tasted all the triumphs and disasters with honesty and appreciation! And, finally, Mary Berry, who I have worked with for nearly 20 years – her support, generous knowledge and encouragement get me through … we laugh and work as though they are one, thank you Mary, you are my inspiration.